BEFORE LAST CALL

How to Increase Your Restaurant's Profitability

STEPHEN A. MASE

ARCHWAY PUBLISHING

Archway Publishing books may be ordered through booksellers or by contacting:

Archway Publishing
1663 Liberty Drive
Bloomington, IN 47403
www.archwaypublishing.com
1 (888) 242-5904

ISBN: 978-1-4808-8669-8 (sc)
ISBN: 978-1-4808-8670-4 (e)

Library of Congress Control Number: 2019921172

Print information available on the last page.

Archway Publishing rev. date: 01/03/2020

Contents

Introduction

In the United States, literally millions of restaurants are operating today, ranging from the highest end of the Michelin rated venues to the grab-and-go concepts that exist all across America. With that many restaurants in operation today, it should not come as any surprise that the restaurant industry pulled in $798 billion, according to 2017 numbers.[1] This was a 4 percent increase from what was the total in 2016, and this growth trend has not stopped.

As people get busier in their day-to-day lives, it is deemed easier to just go out to dinner as opposed to cooking at home. In fact, Americans spend 12.6 percent of their income on food, and 48 percent of that goes to restaurants.[2] In simple terms, people dining out are spending a lot of money. On average, the profit margin of a restaurant is somewhere in the 3 to 5 percent range. With that being said, there are plenty of locations that are struggling to even get to that profitability threshold. Most successful restaurants do not even see an annual profit for at least their first two years due to the myriad of start-up costs that can exist.

---

[1] "Restaurant industry food and drink sales in the United States from 1970 to 2017 (in billion U.S. dollars)", Statista.com, July 29, 2019, 1. https://www.statista.com/statistics/203358/food-and-drinks-sales-of-us-restaurants-since-1970/

[2] "19 Restaurant Statistics Every Restaurateur Should Know", FitSmallBusiness.com, March 27, 2019, 2. https://fitsmallbusiness.com/restaurant-statistics/

While there is nothing wrong with being in the 3 to 5 percent profitability range, I want to see you do better than that. One of the great aspects of the hospitality industry is that there is always room for growth and improvement. I say that being incomplete and always wanting to improve your establishment is a good thing. The moment you stop working to be the best you can be as a restaurant, other locations that continue to work hard and push forward every day will pass you. There are a lot of ways that a restaurant can leak profitability or not maximize their revenue-earning potential. Let me walk you through some of the ways that this can happen and provide you solutions to some of the problems that you might encounter as you work toward maximizing your bottom line.

I have worked in the hospitality industry for over twenty-five years in locations ranging from five-star resorts to what can best be described as a typical dive bar. I have worked in the front of the house (FOH), back of the house (BOH), management, and back office/accounting roles over that time. The hospitality industry is something that has always been a passion of mine, and I have worked very hard to make sure that I know as much as possible about it so I can pass along what I have learned to others in the hopes that they can put that knowledge to use to better their careers. It was only natural that I married my college degree with my love of the hospitality industry to make that my career.

After working for different restaurant groups over the years, I decided it was time to go out on my own and start doing consulting so I could try to reach as many people as possible to help them learn how to do their job at their highest level as it applies to the restaurant industry, primarily focusing on how everything ties back to the profitability of the operation and the financial reporting that accompanies that information.

Most people in the restaurant industry are not accountants, and that's fine. We don't all want to be accountants. Just think about how boring every conversation you have would be if the primary topic in common were accounting. Because not everyone in the industry is fluent in accounting, however, there is a chance that you are just not aware of what a role the accounting can play in all of the day-to-day operations.

Hopefully this book will illustrate to you some areas that you might not know and help make it easier to understand how all of these accounting pieces work together to help create a profitable business. Please see the table of contents as a reference for all of the topics that we will cover. Since some of these topics might be more relevant to you than others are, feel free to skip around from chapter to chapter if you like, but still read the whole book if possible.

If you still have questions after reading this, please feel free to visit my website at www.symmetryrfs.com. I would love to be able to help you maximize your restaurant's profitability, and I am here to help.

CHAPTER 1

So Here You Are in the Hospitality Industry

Owning or running a restaurant or bar is hard work. Anyone who tells you otherwise is not being completely honest with you. A romanticism comes with being in a position of authority in a food and beverage establishment, indicating that there is a good time to be had and, in some cases, this is where the party is.

I'm not saying you cannot have a good time, but if you want to be successful, a lot of hard work is required to achieve your goals of running a profitable establishment. The word *profitable* is open to interpretation, but if you are considering how long it takes to pay off what it costs to open an establishment, a successful location will take about two years to pay it back, while a more typical time frame is usually in the four- to five-year range.

Beyond becoming a profitable location, there is always the looming threat of your restaurant just not making it. Recent studies show that within the first year, the failure rate is close to 60 percent.[3] That is an even higher rate than the divorce rate

---

[3] "The No. 1 thing to consider before opening a restaurant", cnbc.com, updated July 6, 2016, https://www.cnbc.com/2016/01/20/heres-the-real-reason-why-most-restaurants-fail.html

in America right now. Getting past the one-year mark is also no guarantee that your establishment will survive. Numbers show that nearly 80 percent of restaurants and bars close before their five-year mark[4].

If you are constantly running at a loss each year, at some point, your business model is unsustainable, and the restaurant is forced to close. While each restaurant is unique unto itself, there are potential problems common to all restaurants. If you want to succeed, you need to be ready for these issues before they become problems.

One of the first is having the proper start-up capital. Opinions vary as to how much money one should have in reserve to make sure that a restaurant can survive as it gains its footing, but any specific number is arbitrary because all locations are different, and the financial needs for each location are, again, unique.

It is also tough to forecast and speculate what you'll need because you won't know costs at different stages of a year until you actually go through the process. A fair assessment is possible, however, by trying to figure out what the carrying costs for a month will be and then making sure you have enough cash to cover a twelve- to sixteen-month period. In that time, hopefully your location has found its footing and has a good revenue stream working.

Some luck is involved in opening or running a successful restaurant or bar, but a great deal of planning and research also needs to be done in order to maximize the potential for your location. I have seen a restaurant that was just a few weeks away from opening have a fire when lightning struck the location. That is something that you can't plan for, and all of the hard work that

---

[4] "The No. 1 thing to consider before opening a restaurant", cnbc.com, updated July 6, 2016, https://www.cnbc.com/2016/01/20/heres-the-real-reason-why-most-restaurants-fail.html

had been done to get that location to the point that it was close to opening was lost.

I have seen an established location lose half of its revenue-generating potential because someone drove a car through its wall. (We are assuming *that* was not done on purpose.) Half of the restaurant was unusable while construction was being done to repair all of the damage. Those incidents fall under the heading of "bad luck," but most places that collapse are not failing because of occurrences such as those. It's because of avoidable situations. Some of the common reasons include choosing a bad location for your establishment, not knowing who your competition is in the area, and not having a distinct identity for your restaurant.

While there are many other reasons a location may fail, these are examples of causes that can be completely avoided if the proper research and planning are done on the front end. For example, location is a matter of finding a space that works for what you are trying to achieve. Fairly standard questions need to be addressed when looking for a space.

- Is the building big enough for your concept?
- What is the rent per square foot?
- What needs to be built out in the space—booths, bar, kitchen, and so on?
- Is there ample parking?
- What are the demographics of the area?
- What is the average household income in the area?
- Do city ordinances dictate what time you have to close each night?

These are just some of the questions that you need to ask when making sure a space is right for you. If the answers are not what you need them to be, keep looking until you find a site that satisfies all your criteria.

Once you find a location that you believe works for you, get to know your competition. Find out if there are similar restaurant concepts near where you are going to be opening and operating your restaurant. If you are looking to open a coal oven pizzeria, it might be in your best interest not to open that if there is another coal oven pizzeria just two blocks away. It helps to stand out as unique in your immediate area. This way, if someone in your general area wants pizza for dinner, they don't have to make a decision about where to dine.

As a follow-up to picking a location for your restaurant, once you have your concept, stand by it. If you are going to be a coal oven pizzeria, be that, and be the best coal oven pizzeria you can be. It is fine to have other items on the menu that complement your pizza, but stay true to your concept. When guests come to your restaurant, you know what type of food they are there to have.

These sound like simple and obvious observations for opening a restaurant, but if you are trying to launch a concept into an area that is already at its saturation point for that concept, opening a location that is not convenient for people to get to or confuses customers about what your restaurant offers, you are going to be working from a position of weakness to try to get your restaurant up and running.

Another avoidable problem for a restaurant or bar has to do with the product. Obviously you want to serve quality food and beverage products, but that can be easier said than done. One of the biggest hurdles for any restaurant or bar is consistency of product. Regardless of who is in the kitchen or making drinks, you need to make sure that what is being delivered to the guest is made correctly each time.

One of the biggest complaints from guests is that they go to a given restaurant or bar multiple times and, despite ordering the same food or drink as they previously had, what they received was different from the same menu items they have ordered before. Instilling proper training and having the proper recipes for every drink or food menu item that you serve can prevent this type of issue. By doing this, all that is required is that your staff follow directions. As a result, the products have a solid level of consistency.

Maintaining consistency is not solely the responsibility of the bartenders and kitchen staff. It is an important standard for your servers as well. The server staff should know what is on the menu and be able to answer questions about individual items so guests can make the choices that will suit them best for their dining experience.

Regarding drinks, I understand that all servers might not be able to describe to the guests all of the intricacies of a beverage since some people do not drink alcohol and won't be able to test them. At a minimum, however, a server should know what liquors, beers, and wines are carried in the restaurant. But it is not necessarily fair to think that a server would know the exact differences between a pinot noir and a merlot, other than in theory. Depending on the type of restaurant, when these questions do come up, the server can always relay a question to a sommelier or bartender in order to get the best answer to the guest.

The common theme throughout the issue of consistency is training. It is imperative to make sure that all of your employees are trained to their highest level. Several components help to make sure that your employees, either FOH or BOH, are properly trained. Education is one of the primary areas for training. If employees know what is expected of them, then they can do as much studying and practice as they need to get themselves as proficient as possible at their jobs.

For the FOH staff, this includes knowing about the restaurant in general, the clientele, the peak business times, and menu items. If possible, they should know how the dishes are prepared, what possible beverage pairings are (if applicable), how to use the point of sale (POS) system, and what to do if there is any sort of system failure.

For the BOH staff, there is a bit of a different set of standards as it applies to what you would like them to know. Two of the biggest areas of focus in food preparation are speed and accuracy, which need to be maintained while working within the proper food handling guidelines. If your BOH employees are not practicing the proper food handling procedures, it is imperative that someone teaches it to them.

If you are working outside of these guidelines and guests become ill from cross-contamination, you could easily find your kitchen being shut down. If that happens, your chances for operating at your maximum profitability will take a massive hit. In addition to any fines that could be assessed that would hurt your restaurant, you now have a negative reputation, and it will take time and effort to repair that as well. I cannot stress strongly enough the importance of following proper food handling practices.

Assuming that your kitchen is operating with responsible food handling techniques, you want every dish to be prepared exactly the way the guest wants it, and you do not want to keep them waiting too long for their food. With that being the case, the education component is for the kitchen staff to know the menu completely. The better you know how to make each item on the menu without having to refer to any recipes, the quicker you can produce the food. That includes knowing all of the ingredients of the recipes as well as the cook times, proper garnish, and presentation.

Like anything someone wants to get better at, the best way to improve is by repetition and experience. If you are taught to do something correctly and you follow that model, in time you will gain proficiency and speed, which is always a plus in the restaurant industry.

Some employees, however, are able to learn better by seeing how something is done as opposed to just reading about something. That is why another essential piece of training is being able to demonstrate the proper execution of each of the areas of focus for both the FOH and BOH staff. When doing demonstrations for trainees, the trainer needs to make sure they are taking notes and documenting all of the areas of training being covered. They should be following a training manual so there is not a chance that an area is overlooked as it applies to what is being taught.

By following a manual and making sure that the manual is up to date with the latest information, the trainer will know what the trainees should be proficient on as they progress through their training. By keeping track of the training process, the trainer can administer training tests to see how the learning process is going for the trainees.

Another big part of the training structure is that training in constantly ongoing. Training does not end by just learning the ways of the restaurant and how to work effectively when the employee first starts. Constant changes will occur in the restaurant, and it is important to ensure that employees stay current on all of the menu, policies, and software/POS changes as well as anything else that can come up. It is significant that a strong line of communication between the employees and the management exist as well. It is very helpful for the staff to know what they are doing well and what they need to improve on. This is why it is very beneficial to have regular employee reviews and pop quizzes so staff always know what they can improve on.

From that point, make sure that there are always goals for the employees to try to achieve. By setting achievable objectives, you can create standards that will allow you to constantly raise the bar at your establishment. As part of the continued training for your employees, make sure that cross-training is in place so your restaurant has proper coverage even if someone misses a shift. Cross-training also illustrates how each of the positions in the restaurant work in conjunction with one another. The better an employee understands the flow of the work cycle, the better equipped they are to serve their guests.

Training new employees only goes as well as those who are leading the training, and the trainers are only going to be as good as the management that is in place to lead the team. Good managers can be the difference between a restaurant succeeding or failing. In addition to what can be long hours, managers are responsible for creating the staff schedules and handling staff support—filling in as needed, managing inventory, handling guest complaints, ordering products, reviewing product quality, handling daily facility operations, and being the face of the restaurant. (See, I told you this was hard work.) In addition to all of these items—and anything else that I did not include—the managers/owners need to also understand the financial reporting for the restaurant.

Everything that has been listed and discussed so far are items that make an impact on the success or failure of a restaurant. The lifeblood for any restaurant, however, is the customer. You need to give the customer a reason to want to come to your restaurant. You will want your restaurant to be something that is visually pleasing and for the building exterior to draw the customer to want to come in.

Once you have the customer's attention, you can draw them in. Once you draw in the customer, you can draw in their money. The next step is being able to keep the customers coming back. This is where all of the service of the staff and consistency in the food and drink come in to play. Give the guest a reason to want to come back. Make sure that their time in your establishment is memorable for all of the right reasons. If it is, chances are good that your customers will tell others about your restaurant, and the best kind of advertising is word of mouth.

As opposed to reading anonymous posts online about a place or review from a critic, if a friend or an acquaintance of yours tells you about this restaurant that they went to that is something that you just have to try, that carries source credibility because they can tell you all about their experiences in detail, and nothing is better than live testimony.

So hopefully, if you are launching a new restaurant or bar or you have been picked to be the general manager and be the leader and face of an existing establishment, the necessary finances are in place to make sure you have the time to allow your establishment to get the proper traction and draw in plenty of customers.

If it is a new location, let's hope that you have done all of the proper research and planning to secure a convenient location that will maximize the number of guests that you will be able to attract. Let's hope that you have scouted out the competition in the area so you know what you are up against for the customer dollars that are being spent in that marketplace. We are also going to assume that you have put together a good staff consisting of experienced managers, skilled BOH employees, and a pleasant, personable, and knowledgeable FOH team who will give your guests the best experience they can have when they come in to your restaurant. All of that combined with a consistently good product should keep your guests coming back in the future. Add to that progressive staff training and goals for them to keep striving toward, and it will only add to the guests' experiences each time they do come back and increase the chances they will keep returning.

Now that you have a solid customer base and your revenue stream is strong, you need to make sure that you are being fiscally responsible for the well-being of your restaurant. The best tool for being able to do that is your profit and loss statement (P&L).

The majority of people involved in the restaurant and bar industry are there because they like some facet of the business, so they gravitate to that area of the industry because of its appeal.

If you go to culinary school, you do so because you probably want to be a chef. If you go to bartending school, it is probably because you want to be able to put those skills to use working in a restaurant or bar. Most people who want to get into restaurant management will do course work in hospitality management, so they understand what is expected of them in a management role.

The one area I have not yet discussed is the financial aspect of the business. Maybe you are in luck in the fact that there is an accounting person or team who does all of the actual accounting work and you do not have to worry about doing all of the day-to-day accounting functions. Even if you don't have to do the accounting, you will still need to understand how the financial reports work, what is being reported, where the numbers are coming from that make the reports, and how to use this information to better steer your restaurant in the direction that you want or need to go.

Whereas the P&L is an important piece of the puzzle, it is still just one piece of the bigger whole. Your P&L is just a snapshot of a period of time that will show you how your establishment did in that period of time. To truly understand everything that goes into the financial structure of your restaurant business, in addition to knowing where all of the data is coming from, you need to know how it all links together.

One of the biggest problems as it relates to restaurateurs and their financials is that they don't know what they don't know. If you simply do not know what questions to ask, you will probably never get the answers that you are looking for.

At their core, understanding your restaurant's financials are not difficult as they are designed to tell a story. You just need to be equipped to know how to decipher all of the information that is presented and where to look when you have questions. Hopefully this book will help you understand how all of the financial information works together and can aid you manage your business to help you achieve your highest levels of success in your restaurant.

So to recap this chapter, some of the main points that we looked were the following:

- If you are opening a location, taking over as a new manager, or just working at this location, learn what is around you and who your competition is. Know what you need to do to be better than your competition, and then make sure you follow those points of action.
- Training is of vast importance. You can always be better, and you can always be learning. Take advantage of every opportunity to learn more and better your skills.
- Figure out what you do not know and then make it a point to learn and master those areas. Very few people are an expert at everything in a restaurant or bar. The more you learn, the further ahead you will be.
- This will be hard work, so be ready to work hard.

CHAPTER 2

Don't Be Afraid of Your Profit and Loss Statement

The majority of people in the United States do not have an accounting degree. In fact, based on numbers from 2018, only about 0.8 percent of people in the United States work in a job that is an accounting-related position.[5] [6]In truth, numbers are not for everyone when it comes to doing your job. This applies to the restaurant industry as much as any other field of occupation.

Depending on what you do for your restaurant, there might not be a need for you to have to understand all the numbers that get moved around and discussed. In some cases, however, knowing what all the numbers mean is critical to how the business is run and the decision-making that accompanies that information. At the end of each reporting period, whether it be weekly, a twenty-eight-day period, each calendar month, or quarterly, a

[5] "How many people are currently employed as Accountants and Auditors in the Untied States", Studentscholarships.org, accessed July 16, 2019, https://studentscholarships.org/professions/570/employed/accountants_and_auditors.php#sthash.l52E3CGA.dpb

[6] "Labor Force in the United States", Wikipedia.com, accessed July 16, 2019, https://en.wikipedia.org/wiki/Labor_force_in_the_United_States

P&L should be produced so the restaurant will know how well it did overall and in comparison to the budget that was in place.

Your P&L is comprised of three main parts: the revenue, the cost of goods sold, and the expenses. If you take all of the revenue and subtract all of the cost of goods sold, you will come up with your gross profit. If you subtract all of the remaining expenses from the gross profit, you will arrive at your net income (or loss) for the reporting period.

That is the report in its very simplest concept. It is much more detailed than that, but to arrive at what you made or lost for the reporting period, that is the math used. We will go through every piece of the P&L, however, so it is easy to see how we arrive at this finish line.

The first portion of your statement is the revenue section. This represents all of the profits that are earned from selling food, beverages, or retail items to your guests. How this is displayed on your statement is entirely up to you, but at a minimum, you need to separate the food sales from the beverage sales from any other type of retail sales. Within the food category of the revenue, you might want to then separate the lunch sales from the dinner sales, as well as breakfast and late-night sales, if those apply.

On the beverages side, you will want to separate out the liquor, beer, and wine sales so you can see how much of each you have sold, if that is applicable. The more distinction you have in what category the sales belong in, the more information you will be able to gather from your P&L as it applies to your food and beverage cost percentages, labor percentages, and controllable costs. Any of the retail merchandise that gets purchased will be recorded as part of your revenue, but it needs to be again sectioned off from the food and beverage purchases because you do not want to include this revenue source with the food or beverage sales so you are not distorting your food and beverage costs.

Working against the revenue number will be the cost of

goods sold (COGS), and as stated above, the gross profit is the revenue minus the COGS. The COGS is simply what is spent to purchase all of the food and ingredients and/or beverages that are used to produce the food and/or drinks sold to the guests. The cost is figured by taking the beginning inventory value and adding the purchases made in the period that is being reported and subtracting out the closing inventory value. Having the revenue and the COGS also will help you get to the cost percentage for food and beverages, but we will look at that process closer a little while later. The top portion of your P&L should look similar to the following in its format:

Sales - Food	$131,202.25
Sales - Sundries	$4.00
Sales - Non Alch Beverage	$750.00
Sales - Wine	$47,520.00
Sales - Liquor	$15,916.00
Sales - Beer	$1,616.00
Sales - Returns	$0.00
Total Sales	$197,008.25
COS - Food	$42,007.51
COS - Wine	$6,020.70
COS - Liquor Shrinkage	$7,571.62
COS - Beer	$234.74
Total COS	$55,834.57
Gross Profit	$141,173.68

As mentioned previously, your P&L can be much more specific in showing the sales broken down by when these sales occur so you can see what percentage of your sales are lunch, dinner, or other. By splitting apart the revenues, you will be able to see what percentage of sales are done within each mealtime. This becomes important when working around the labor cost percentages to make sure you are staffing correctly to maximize your labor dollars spent. To make sure that all of your revenue is reporting correctly, you may want to make sure that what is reporting as your revenues in your accounting program match what is being reported on your daily sales reports (DSRs) for the same period of time.

If there is a difference between the two totals when looked at for the same periods of time, this would indicate that there is a mapping issue with data coming into the system if there is a direct import from your POS system into your accounting software. If you enter your data manually, then there is a chance that some data got posted to an incorrect account line.

A simple rule to follow is that your DSR, if in balance, is the source document that you need to rely on regarding your sales numbers. This is the source document because this data is pulled directly out of the POS system, so this accounts for everything that was rung in throughout the day.

If there are no interruptions that would cause the POS system to lose power or have to reset and all of the open checks are closed out properly, all of the sales should match all of the payments. If you have an auto-import function set up that moves the data of the daily sales in the POS directly to your accounting system and you know that it is in balance, you can post that data. If you have open checks that were not able to be closed or there was some sort of service interruption, it is possible that the system will come back up and not be in balance due to an open check not being able to be closed. Most systems will alert you that the DSR is out of balance, and you will need to make an entry to correct that so you can post the daily sales.

Now that you have an understanding about how the revenues

and gross profits are figured, the other part of the P&L is the expenses. Most P&Ls have at least the following categories that make up their expenses: labor, operating, marketing, utilities, general and administrative, occupancy, and other/corporate. Within each of these categories, there is a breakdown so each expense can be individualized. The decision to how much detail there is in the breakdown is completely up to the person who is in charge of the restaurant reporting, but the more specification, the better. The key to making all of this work, however, is that everything must be coded and mapped correctly so the proper expenses are showing up in the correct category.

We will start with the labor component. For the breakdown of labor costs, you will want to separate the FOH and BOH labor, as these represent very different areas of the labor. Here is an example of what your BOH labor breakdown might look like:

Kitchen	$6,638.27
Kitchen OT	$1,127.33
Kitchen Training	$250.00
Expo	$500.00
Utility	$2,509.23
Utility OT	$527.40
Utility Training	$200.00
Temporary Labor	$150.00
Casual Labor	$0.00
Direct BOH Labor	$11,902.23

This is a good representation of everything that could make up your BOH labor broken down to show what makes up the regular hours, the overtime hours, and training hours for all of the BOH components. There are different designations of a certain labor category (like dishwasher) because there are different labor codes for what an employee is being paid for. Usually, when an employee is in training, that person is going to be paid at a training rate, so those need to be reflected. In addition, since overtime is paid at a time-and-a-half rate, we need to see how much overtime is being paid. This can be an indicator as it applies to being able to see if there is proper scheduling being done to try to maximize employee's work hours without running overtime rates. The same breakdown would hold true for the FOH labor:

Servers	$1,337.97
Servers OT	$4.61
Servers Training	$0.00
Asst. Servers	$968.60
Asst Serv OT	$175.62
Asst Serv Training	$0.00
Bar	$950.50
Bar OT	$6.47
Bar Training	$200.00
Wine Steward	$1,101.75
Host	$2,228.85
Cashier	$125.35
Cashier OT	$0.00
Host/Door	$0.00
Host Training	$0.00
Direct FOH Labor	$7,099.72

The key is to make sure that you are identifying what makes up the regular hours, the overtime hours, and any training hours. This goes back to the payroll process and the clocking in and out process that the employees every shift needs to do. Then the managers need to check to make sure the hours look correct for each shift. The FOH and BOH labor is only for the employees who clock in and out. The managers for both FOH and BOH do not get included in these labor totals. Since the managers are on salary, they do not count against the labor percentages, as they are in a separate category of expense for management labor. Depending on how you have your P&L set up, that can be a separate section to show all management labor or just a separate line item.

Management labor does not count against the labor percentages for a couple of reasons. If you had a manager who does some FOH coverage, a little bit of BOH coverage, and then some administrative work, to be able to allocate the amount of time and expense that was spent in each area would be very difficult to properly represent. Also, and more importantly, the labor percentages are to gauge the employees who clock in and out and are not on salary.

Since managers are usually on salary, you would have a misrepresentation of value for their time worked. As most manager's hourly rate of pay is greater than a BOH employee, it would skew the labor percentage to the high side quickly as well. Finally, the number of hours that a manager worked are usually going to be greater than a typical BOH employee. If the kitchen either closes down or cuts back to a late-night menu at midnight but the bar stays open until 2:00 a.m., a manager should still be in the restaurant to run the business up until closing that night, so it would not be a proper reflection of how the labor hours were spent unless labor allocations were made.

Now that we have looked at the revenue, the COGS, and the labor portions of the P&L, this is a good time to talk about cost percentages. Percentages usually examine three areas: food cost, beverage cost, and labor cost. These areas are looked at more on a percentage basis as opposed to the overall dollars spent or variance to the budget because these percentages are based off the revenue for the reporting period, so there is a direct correlation between what the revenue is and the money spent.

If the revenue is exceptionally strong and well in excess of what the budget had called for, it stands to reason that the labor hours will be greater based on the demand and the purchases for food and beverages will be greater than the budget had called for because of the increase in business. The focal point is going to remain on the concept of "Did the expenses remain in the proper percentage ratio as what the budget called for?"

The way that the percentages for food cost is calculated is that you take the COGS and divide that by the food sales. For example, if your cost of goods was $4,250 for food and your sales were $20,000, your food cost would be 21.25 percent. If your cost of goods were $8,500 and your sales were $40,000, you would still be running the 21.25 percent food cost (which would make any manager happy).

So even if you were budgeted to have $6,500 for your COGS for food, it is fine that you exceeded that number as the increased revenue kept the percentage in a good place. The same calculation applies when figuring out the beverage cost, but there is one exception when figuring out beverage costs that does not apply to food.

Liquor, beer, and wine are all considered beverage, but they are three very distinct categories, whereas food cost constitutes all food. Once you know your food cost for the reporting period, you can break that number down based on the COGS for each of the areas that food is categorized as: meat, dairy, produce, seafood, nonalcoholic, and other (any food that does not obviously belong to one of the named categories).

That usually is not needed for reporting purposes because on the revenue side of the P&L the line is listed for food sales. So since all food sales are combined into that line, all the COGS are just thought of as food. For the beverage cost, however, since the revenue is usually broken out to show liquor, beer, and wine sales, it is easy to figure out the cost of sales for each of the beverage categories since the purchases for each liquor, beer, and wine are represented on your P&L in the COGS section.

When figuring out the labor cost, you are working with the total sales number when it comes to calculating the labor percentages as opposed to figuring out the food and beverage percentage where the COGS number is divided by the specific revenue for that COGS category. The following is a look at an example of what a condensed P&L showing just the labor portion would look like.

	Actual	%	Budget	%
Sales - Food	$180,072.75	67.78%	$169,825.85	69.98%
Sales - Wine	$61,422.50	23.12%	$49,851.90	20.54%
Sales - Liquor	$21,551.00	8.11%	$20,096.15	8.28%
Sales - Beer	$2,626.00	0.99%	$2,915.10	1.20%
Total Sales	$265,672.25	100.00%	$242,689.00	100.00%
Kitchen	$7,813.69	2.94%	$8,231.98	3.39%
Kitchen OT	$689.82	0.26%	$242.12	0.10%
Kitchen Training	$0.00	0.00%	$0.00	0.00%
Utility	$3,645.72	1.37%	$3,147.52	1.30%
Utility OT	$396.38	0.15%	$242.12	0.10%
Utility Training	$0.00	0.00%	$0.00	0.00%
Temp Labor	$0.00	0.00%	$0.00	0.00%
Direct BOH Labor	$12,545.61	4.72%	$11,863.74	4.89%
Servers	$1,623.96	0.61%	$1,936.94	0.80%
Servers OT	$100.63	0.04%	$169.48	0.07%
Servers Training	$93.20	0.04%	$435.81	0.18%
Asst. Servers	$1,680.25	0.63%	$1,452.70	0.60%
Asst Serv OT	$144.71	0.05%	$121.06	0.05%
Asst Serv Training	$441.18	0.17%	$121.06	0.05%
Bar	$1,184.65	0.45%	$1,210.59	0.50%
Bar OT	$91.48	0.03%	$72.64	0.03%
Bar Training	$0.00	0.00%	$48.42	0.02%
Wine Steward	$183.00	0.07%	$980.77	0.40%
Host	$1,474.00	0.55%	$1,951.92	0.80%
Host OT	$0.00	0.00%	$0.00	0.00%
Host/Door	$0.00	0.00%	$0.00	0.00%
Host Training	$0.00	0.00%	$0.00	0.00%
Direct FOH Labor	$7,017.06	2.64%	$8,501.38	3.50%

As you can see, even though the dollar amounts for the BOH labor is greater than what is budgeted, it is still within the proper parameters because the overall percentages for both the FOH and BOH labor are lower than what was budgeted. This is because the revenue for the reporting period was also greater than what was budgeted.

Due to the fact that everything for food, beverage, and labor costs are looked at in relation to what the revenue was for the reporting period, that is why the focus for these three areas is based on percentages versus actual dollars spent. If the revenue is lower than expected, then the COGS and the labor needs to be scaled down. If the revenue is greater than expected, then it is safe to assume that the COGS and labor dollars spent is going to be greater than what was budgeted.

The remainder of your P&L will be comprised of the remaining expenses that are incurred in the reporting period. The normal categories that are included in the expenses are, but not limited to, employee benefits, operating expenses, marketing, utilities, administrative and general, occupancy, and corporate/depreciation. Of these expense categories, the area that the restaurant manager has the most influence over is the operating expenses. These are the items that the manager has the most influence on because these are expenses that are incurred because someone directly made a purchase for something that was needed as opposed to a cost just being a recurring monthly expense.

For example, there is a cost to replacing the table linens as needed. If the restaurant is very busy, then you will need to order more linens, and the cost will be on the high end. Conversely, if the restaurant is having a slow month, the need for linens will be lessened, thus keeping the expense for the month down.

The following is a list of items that could commonly show up as operating expenses: laundry and linen, uniforms, silverware, chinaware, glassware, utensils, dish machine supplies, janitorial supplies, paper supplies, kitchen/dining/bar supplies, dining room supplies, bar supplies, menus and wine lists, alarm services, valet services, police services, cleaning services, food safety inspections, knife sharpening, landscaping, research and development (food tastings), armored car, pest control, other services, equipment rental, flowers and decorations, printing and office supplies, music, and repair and maintenance.

Based on the needs of your restaurant, some of these items would not apply, but these are all expenses that the ordering manager would have control over ordering on a monthly basis so there should never be any surprises when reviewing a P&L as to where some of the expenses came from. The remaining expenses that fill out the P&L are items that are either recurring expenses or going to occur without someone having to specifically order them and receive an invoice that needs to be paid.

For the utilities, these would include gas, electric, waste removal, cable, internet access, telephone, and water, to name a few. These are bills that the restaurant can do very little about in regards to whether or not you have to have these services. Occupancy expenses are centered around rent, percentage rent (if applicable), CAM charges, property taxes, and parking, to name a few. Again, these items are pretty much a given each month unless there is some sort of deal that is struck that would waive the rent, for example.

The expenses that fall under the category of administrative and general include such things as bank charges, credit card commissions, postage, licenses and permits, comps, travel expenses, and general insurance. Again, all these items will show up as expenses on a monthly basis, and very little can be done so any of these charges do not occur on a monthly cycle. So as stated earlier, your P&L consists of your revenue minus your COGS to arrive at your gross profit.

Now that you have all of your monthly expenses, you can

figure out how to arrive at your net operating income (NOI). All you have to is subtract all of the aforementioned expenses from the gross profit and you have your NOI. And hopefully it is a positive number. If your NOI is not where you would like it to be, it could be that your revenue came in lower than anticipated or your expenses were higher than expected. There are ways to solve these problems, and if you keep reading, you will see some solutions.

Finally, one more component needs to be included, the corporate overhead expenses that need to get added in. There is nothing that the operations team can do regarding these expenses as these will exist no matter what measures are taken. The types of expenses included in this category are accounting fees, management fees, other professional fees, interest expense, and general corporate expenses. These expenses are subtracted from the NOI to give you a net income (or loss) number that is the bottom-line number of your financial statement.

This is all there is to the P&L for your restaurant. The key is to make sure that you have everything that occurred in the reporting period included in this statement. That will allow you to know what your bottom-line profit or loss is while also informing you about the cost percentages for your food, beverage, and labor categories.

The final piece to you feeling confident with your P&L is the format of the report itself. Some people have no issues reading the statements while others may have trouble with the optics of how the report is laid out. Most accounting software programs will provide options of what you can select to show on your P&L, and this will allow you to look at the current data for the reporting period and compare that to either the budget, a prior period, or the same period in a prior year. Also included would be a column that will show percentages for each line item on the report.

The percentages that show up on the P&L signify different things depending on which portion of the P&L you are looking at. For the sales/revenue section of the P&L, the percentages that are listed for food, liquor, beer, and wine will total up to 100 percent as these percentages are showing what the ratio of sales is for each of the revenue categories.

In the COGS section, the listed percentages are what your food cost, liquor, beer, and wine (or total beverage) costs are for the reporting period. For all of the remaining expenses, the percentage number represents the expense divided by the total sales amount. This tells you what percent each expense is of the total sales. This information then comes in handy as it applies to creating budgets.

In addition to the reports that can be generated out of your accounting system, most systems should also allow you to be able to export your reports to an Excel format so you can customize your reporting setup so it is the easiest for you to read. As mentioned above, to truly give your report all of the comparative information, you will want to show the current period data versus the current budget and then include the information from the same period from the prior year, the year-to-date cumulative total, the year-to-date budget, and the prior year-to-date information. With each of those, there will also be the corresponding percentage information. So the header of each of the columns on your P&L would look something like this:

Actual	%	Budget	%	Prior Year	%	YTD Actual	%	YTD Budget	%	Prior YTD

By having these different columns of data, you will be able to compare how you are doing versus what you were expecting to do (budget) and how you did a year previously (prior year) for the same time period for both a single reporting period and the cumulative year to date.

This covers the basic principles of your P&L and how to read it. It is important to understand where the data comes from that generates the numbers that populate the statement. Once you have that figured out, you are able to see the flow of information and track how your restaurant is doing. The next step in the process of understanding your statement is to be able to look into each account line that makes up the P&L and see the detail that creates the figures on each line.

Most accounting software program do have the option to drill in to each line of your P&L by just clicking on the line, and this will take you to the general ledger information, the detail that makes up the numbers that populate the statement. By being able to look at the detail for each account line, you will know if everything is classified to the correct line for accurate reporting, and if it is not, you will know what you have to move so all items are classified to the proper place.

That is a general overview of what makes up your income statement and how the numbers and percentages are arrived at. Not everyone is a numbers person, and trying to understand how this process works if you have had no training or explanation can be intimidating.

Don't be afraid. These numbers just reflect how the restaurant did financially for a particular reporting period. The more time you spend reading and interpreting these reports, the more you will come to understand that these reports tell a story, not just how you have done but also where you are headed.

Working in the operations side of the business, a manager should be able to see the correlation between how busy the restaurant was and how well the restaurant did on the NOI for the reporting period. With the proper training and experience, you will be able to run a restaurant that will maximize its returns because you will have all of the knowledge needed to always know how the restaurant is doing financially every step of the way.

So to put a bow on this section, what did we learn about the P&L? We wanted to focus on the following:

- The P&L tells a story for a set period of time that you are choosing to look at. Learn to be able to read this data as it applies to not only the reporting period you are looking at, but in comparison to the budget, the prior reporting periods, as well as the prior year.
- Know what makes up the different section of your P&L (revenue, cost of goods, and expenses) and where all of the information that make up the numbers on the report come from and how they are generated.
- Understand that the percentages for cost (food, beverage, and labor) are looked more so than just the actual gross numbers and learn how to control these percentages if they are too high.

CHAPTER 3

The Importance of Account Reconciliation

One of the most basic and important cornerstones to accounting at any level is the reconciling of accounts. This is simply a process that proves out and documents that account balances are tied out and, as needed, match up to source documentation. This can apply to different sections of the accounting process, but each has its own importance.

For your cash accounts, it is important to make sure that you can tie back to your bank statements. For your expense accounts, it is vital to make sure that all of your expenses are coded properly and reporting to the correct expense line. On your balance sheet, it is important that you can tie back all of your line items to activity from period to period. This would include being able to tie back lines such as your accounts payable, accounts receivable, accruals, and prepaid items to match up with source documents like the corresponding invoices (incoming and outgoing) and payment schedules.

Whereas reconciliation of all accounts is an important task, making sure that the cash accounts are correct might be the most significant as this will also help to determine that the daily sales are reporting properly. Each day the POS system should generate a DSR that will show a breakdown of all of the sales and payments. The sales data can be customized to show the detail of the day's activity in whatever manner you would like—showing lunch and dinner separately and dividing out liquor, beer, and wine individually—and any other purchase that may have been made for that day, like a gift card or any merchandise that may be sold at the restaurant. Here is an example of the information and format that you would see in a DSR:

Visa	$2,035.48
Mastercard	$220.97
Amer. Express	$547.57
Discover	$21.49
Total credit card	$2,825.51
room charges	$0.00
deposits taken	$0.00
applied deposits	$0.00
taxes	$222.68
food revenue	$1,978.75
NA beverage	$48.75
Liquor revenue	$199.00
Beer Revenue	$719.65
Wine Revenue	$106.00
Total Sales	$3,052.15
Gift card purchase	
Gift card redeem	-$8.10
open discounts	
employee food	$148.63
manager meals	$416.70

did not like	$12.25
kitchen error	
server error	
owner comp	
marketing	$82.75
Total Comps	$660.33
Admin fees	$64.00
tip out	$12.15
cash due	-$142.96
debits	$3,342.88
credits	$3,342.88

The payments will be broken out into a few different categories to show what method of payment was used. There should be a section that shows that cash the was rung in, as well as the breakdown of what was charged to each type of credit card (Visa, MasterCard, American Express, etc.). Beyond those categories, there should be account lines for any types of comps that are used, as comps are, theoretically, a form of payment. The difference with comps is that the house is making a payment for something as opposed to the guest.

You might also see lines for payments to house accounts or the use of gift cards to tender payment, if applicable. The key to all of these forms of payment is that everything has a designated home, and there should not be any forms of payment that are just listed as miscellaneous payment or income.

So now that the POS system has created this detail of a day's activity, this needs to be entered into your accounting system. This can be done in one of two ways:

1. Your accounting system might have an interface module that is active between the POS system and the accounting system where the data is just automatically imported from the POS system.

2. If this does not exist, then the best way to enter this information is to just do a journal entry and book all of that data in on a daily basis.

The key to each of these entries, whether it be done automatically or by hand, is that the sales and the payments need to match up to the same amount. For most systems that can do the import, the system will make sure that the two sides (sales and payments) of the entry balance, or else the entry cannot be posted. If you have to do the entry manually, your debits and credits should equal the same amount. If they do not, you will need to make sure that you do not have something categorized backwards (a debit as a credit or vice versa). If that is not the case, then it is possible that there is something that is not reporting out of the POS system properly. That would mean that you would need to look at the mapping to make sure that everything that needs to be reported on a DSR is in fact getting reported out of the POS system.

Once this is done and all of the data from the DSR is out of the POS system and into your accounting system, you will be able to reconcile your cash and credit cards, as well as any payments that come out of your system as well. Every accounting system I have ever worked on has a form of a cash reconciliation report as part of the program. The way this works is that as the data gets entered into the system, the cash coming in will be designated as the debits and any payments leaving the system will be listed as a credit.

As for what is constituted as cash, that is based on how your system is set up with its mapping to determine what is being reported. The most common breakdown of this is to have the credit cards that are being processed split into the groups of who the processor is handling. The most common setup is that there is American Express payments separate from all of the other credit cards that your restaurant accepts (Visa, Mastercard, Discover, etc.), and then there is the actual cash that is used. So on a given day, you would see three entries in the debit column, something for cash, American Express, and the remaining credit cards that are accepted.

On the other side of the reconciliation report would be the credits. As previously stated, this would be all of the payments that are coming out of the restaurant. This would include all of the checks that were issued, as well as the bookings for any other types of payments that are made, like payroll, or any items that are set up on some sort of auto-pay function, like your utilities, for example. There will also be any miscellaneous items that would need to be booked as journal entries for any payments that go out, like a refund to a guest's credit card or any payments that would ever be made over the phone to a vendor. Between the cash activity from the guest that is coming in and payables that are going out, this should represent all of the activity that is occurring within the operating account for the restaurant.

The act of reconciling your bank account(s) will then serve several functions:

1. You will be able to make sure that all of the cash and credit card amounts that are being reported through your DSR is correct.
2. You will be able to make sure that all of your recurring monthly expenses are posting properly.
3. You will be able to have a working cash flow for your restaurant because you will know that everything is posting as it should.

Not everyone has the time or the need to reconcile your cash accounts on a daily basis, but if it is possible, it is highly advantageous to do so. Also, if reconciliations are done on a daily basis, the amount of time it takes is less than trying to do weeks, or a full month, of reconciliation at one time.

Doing an actual reconciliation of a cash account is not difficult, and depending on the amount of activity that has taken place, it can also be done in a short period of time. The first step of the process is to access the bank account you are looking to reconcile. If you are able to print up the bank activity for the period of time that you are going to be reconciling, that is even better.

Once you have that account data, you will need to go into the reconciliation program in your accounting system. The system will ask you to choose the account you want to reconcile, and once you do that, you will be asked to enter the closing balance of that account. Once that amount is entered, you will be taken to a screen that shows all of the activity that has been posted for the debits and credits.

In order to reconcile an account in your system, you will simply need to go through the list of entries on the bank statement and just click the check box for each entry that is on the bank statement, as that should match what is in your system. A line in the reconciliation program will show if the reconciliation is in balance or not. Once all of the activity from the statement is checked off, the balance should read as a $0 amount. If there is an existing balance, then either something has not been checked off or needs to be entered so it can be.

By doing this exercise every day, you will be able to prove out a few different areas, which will help to make sure that all of the data in your system is correct or to see if there is anything related to the transactions that need to be looked at. The actual cash deposits taken in each day at the restaurant will need to go to the bank on a regular rotation. It is important to keep each day's cash deposit amount separate so it is easy to see the amount on the bank statement and match those amounts up to what is in the reconciliation program. If there is a discrepancy, it is very easy to see these if this is being done on a regular basis.

For example, if the DSR indicates that the cash deposit for the day should have been $870.31, that is the amount that should be showing up on the bank statement. If the amount that shows up on the bank statement is $885.31, that would mean that there was an overage (for any number of reasons), and there would need to be an entry made in to the system for the $15 so the system can be balanced. The same logic would apply if the amount that is showing on the bank statement is less than what the DSR would indicate is the proper amount. Let's say that there was a counter-feit $20 bill in the cash deposit and the bank only recognized a deposit of $850.31. An entry would have to be made in order to account for that bad bill so the system can be balanced.

In addition to just any normal overage or shorting of the theoretical deposit (what the system says is the cash due for the day), if there is a constant differential between what is deposited and what is due to be deposited, it could just be a matter of theft. One of the best ways to look into this as an option is to do an audit of the safe to see how much money is actually in the safe and see if that matches what the total is supposed to be. If the amount stored in the safe does not reconcile to what the balance sheet indicates the balance should be, then there should be some other information that would explain the differential. If that does not exist, there will need to be controls and follow-up put in place to make sure that there is not theft occurring.

By doing the reconciliation, you will know as soon as possible if there is anything that is incorrect about your cash deposits. The longer you might wait to do the reconciliation, the more difficult it becomes to account for any discrepancies, unless someone on the operations side is keeping meticulous records of every dollar that might be over or short as it applies to the actual deposit versus what the system (or theoretical) deposit is stated to be.

When dealing with the actual cash, you should know when the money is going to the bank so you will know when that is available to be seen on a bank statement and then be able to be cleared off a reconciliation page. The same mentality also exists for the credit card amounts that are processed to your bank. These amounts should also match what is on the DSR, but for credit cards, there is a clearing process that does take a couple of days, as that is the normal rotation of funds when working through a credit card processor.

As it applies to the credit card processing, a few techniques make it easier to reconcile these amounts as they show up on a bank statement. Most credit card processing companies offer different options of how you would prefer to have your processing fees taken out. There is the option to have fees taken out on a daily basis or to have all of the fees taken out once a month on a monthly cycle. When getting your credit card process set up, you should ask for the credit card fees to be taken from the account on a monthly basis.

The main difference between the two is that the daily fees are deducted from what the amount is that is going to post to your account each day. The once-a-month fees will show up as a line item on your bank statement as a deduction. This is helpful because the amount that your DSR reports each day is the amount that should show up in your bank account.

For example, if there is an amount for your Visa/Mastercard processing for the day that should be $15,892.75, per your DSR, that is what should show up on the bank statement. If there are fees taken out, then the amount would be lower by an unspecified amount. By knowing what the fee percentage is, you can get a good idea of what would be a reasonable amount to have for fees, but not an exact amount, as that is something that varies based on the types of cards used for payment. The problem with this would be if there are any other charges that would be included in an amount that was coming out against your DSR total.

For example, say there was $482.47 in credit card fees for the day, but there was also a guest refund of $50 to a credit card that you were not aware of. The total that would show on the bank statement for the credit card payments would be $15,360.28. Your natural inclination would be that the difference of $532.47 would need to be booked to credit card merchant fees, and this would be a reasonable amount. This would be a reconciling item, and you would move forward as everything would properly tie out. The problem would be that you misrepresented that $50.

If the fees came out once a month, then you would know that if there were a $50 variance between your DSR amount and your bank statement amount for that specific day, that someone else did some sort of activity to make that amount change. It is much easier to identify any items when they stand alone. It also saves a great deal of time as you would know immediately to ask questions since the two numbers do not match.

Another item to keep an eye on when reconciling credit card amounts is that it is not uncommon for a couple of day's activities to be combined when dealing with weekends or holidays. When that occurs, it is usually just a matter of adding the total of two or more days together from the DSR information. This would match the amount that is showing on a bank statement. If there is a discrepancy, it is a bit more difficult to pin down exactly what day a refund would be posting, but as long as it can be determined the exact amount of a refund, that would just need to be booked as a credit and will allow you to balance to zero.

It is also important to keep in mind that if there are any sort of deposits made via credit card, these amounts will just be part of an amount that shows on a bank statement. For example, on the day that you had $15,892.75 show up on the DSR, if the bank statement had a total of $17,392.75, you would be out of balance by $1,500. This would serve as a reminder to ask if anyone took a deposit of $1,500. Then that would need to be booked accordingly and cleared as well. If the reconciling process only takes place every several weeks, trying to get answers to all activity that may have happened weeks ago can take much longer than something that might have happened only a few days ago.

When dealing with the credit side of the reconciliation process, this is much more specific, as either an amount occurred or it didn't. There are not many ways that an amount can be different than what is in the system, as opposed to the additions or subtractions that can occur with the debits.

For example, if there is check #1245 that was for $5,500 for rent, the only amount that check should be able to clear for is the $5,500. If on the bank statement it was to show check #1245 clearing for any amount other than the $5,500, then it is either a bank error or a level of fraud is taking place. The same logic would apply for any payments that are made either by an auto-pay function or when funds are impounded. The latter would apply to the way most payroll companies handle their payment functions.

So that is the process of how a bank reconciliation would work. It is simply a matter of looking at a bank statement and checking off all of the items that cleared for a specific day—both debits and credits. By doing so, you will always know what your current reconciled balance is, which is important, as well as knowing if there is any fraud or malfeasance that may be taking place. By doing this on a daily basis, it creates a good check and balance between the accounting side of the restaurant and the operations side.

If done properly, in addition to knowing what the reconciled balance of your account is, you will also be able to tell what your book balance is. The difference between the two is that the book balance is including all of the deposits in transit (both cash and credit card) because that money is yours and is going to be show-ing up in the bank. It just has not made it there at the time you are doing your reconciliation.

Reconciling the cash account(s) as regularly as possible is a good practice, but it is not the only set of accounts that need to be tied out. As mentioned earlier, there are expense accounts and balance sheet accounts that need to be reconciled regularly. The timing and urgency in which these accounts need to be reconciled, however, is more a function of how often financial statements are produced.

For this exercise, we will say that the financial reports are produced on a monthly cycle. With that being the case, the ex-penses entered through the accounts payable process have specific account codes that are used to route the expenses to their correct home. Since this is usually a manual process, there is always the risk that an error in coding could occur. There is also the case where there is an expense that could be classified as one of several different expense codes.

For example, you could have an invoice that is for cleaners and cleansers, and that could be categorized as cleaning supplies, bar supplies, or janitorial supplies. The best thing to do is to see where other invoices were coded before from this vendor. If there is a consistency that is maintained, at least there is a pattern that can be followed as to why something is coded as it was. Proper payables coding is part of the accounts payable process, which we will be looking at soon.

Not to be overly repetitive, but this chapter had a very direct message:

- Reconcile your bank accounts as often as possible. If your cash is reporting correctly, the remaining parts of your daily sales information will probably be correct as this data cannot be posted if it does not balance. Also if you see something is out of line with your cash, it is easier to fix it the quicker you catch it being wrong.

- Cash accounts are not the only accounts that need to be reconciled. All accounts need to be looked at to make sure that they are all reflecting proper information.
- By making sure that your cash accounts are correct, you will be able to have a better handle on your cash management.

CHAPTER 4

What Makes Up the Expenses of Your Profit and Loss Statement

Your P&L is broken down in to two discernable sections: the revenues (which, when you take out the COGS, gives you your gross profit) and your expenses. The expenses on your P&L are broken down into several categories, and those are brought into your system in a couple of different manners. The categories of expenses include, but are not limited to, labor expenses, employee benefits, direct expenses, repair and maintenance, advertising/ public relations, promotions, comps, building costs, utilities, general and administrative, management fees, and other.

Your list of expenses can be a little more detailed if you desire, depending on how specific you want to have them be. Conversely, expense categories can also be condensed to be just a single line item. For example, for repair and maintenance expenses, you could split out items such as plumbing, electrical, HVAC, and so forth, or it could be just listed as repair and maintenance to cover all of those expenses.

There are three common ways that the expenses will get posted and show up on the P&L. Those are through the entry of invoices into the accounting system, the booking of entries to post transactions that take place (like your payroll), and recurring entries. Recurring entries are also done primarily through journal entries, but the recurring entries could be a result of a prepaid item that has been amortized, loan payments, and rent, to name a few.

Usually within your accounting software, you can set up any recurring entries to be auto-created, and all you would need to do is review and post those entries each reporting period. The most common way that the expenses get into your system is through the entry of invoices. The majority of the invoices that you will receive will most likely be coming from your food and beverage vendors, as that is the business you are in.

Each restaurant will have its own method of how their invoices are reviewed and processed, but here is a general idea of how this process should work.

1. The process will start with product being ordered and then delivered.
2. When the delivery shows up, whomever the company's designated person is to handle the receiving of orders needs to check it in.
3. The delivery driver should have a copy of the invoice for what is being delivered. A copy of that invoice should be reviewed by the person that receives the order to make sure that everything listed on the invoice is indeed delivered.
4. In addition to making sure that all of the ordered product was delivered, any perishable items should also be checked for their freshness by the person who receives the order to ensure you have not received any product that has gone bad.
5. Once the order is confirmed as being correct, the person who received the order needs to sign off on the invoice and then code the order for accounting purposes.

The coding process allows an invoice to be entered into the accounting system and show up in the correct expense line. The coding itself is simply assigning the proper expense account to each item on an invoice. This goes back to the chart of accounts that is in place for your company. (Please refer to the appendix for an example chart of accounts.) For each specific type of item, a separate account code is used so all of the expenses will show up in the proper expense classification.

When doing the coding, the best practice is that the person who either does the receiving of the product or the person who actually placed the order should do the coding. This is the best practice because there is a firsthand knowledge of what was ordered and why, so that is the best person to do the coding.

For the most part, when dealing with food and beverage invoices, the coding is rather straightforward. Most chart of accounts have all of their food broken down to cover all of the different categories that food products fall in to. This would include meat, poultry, seafood, dairy, produce, nonalcoholic, and general/ other. The "general" category would cover items such as spices, seasonings, and any other items that would not fit exactly into any of the other categories.

Again, the main reason that it is helpful for the person who does the ordering to do the coding is that they know why the products were ordered, so they know how to code them properly so they show up on the P&L on the proper line.

For example, let's say that your restaurant is working on a few new menu items for some barbequed meats. Since there will be some level of testing to make sure the cook times and temperatures are proper, as well as ensuring that all of the seasonings are done in the correct proportions, some trial runs will be done to make sure that the finished product is exactly what is desired.

During these trials, the ordered meat should not be categorized as a meat purchase because it is not for sale to the customer.

This should not be part of the expense that goes to any sort of food cost. This would need to go to a research and development (R&D) expense line. The person who would know what exactly is being used for R&D would be the person who placed the order, so that is why it is best to have them do the coding. This cuts down on any sort of speculation if another person were doing the coding.

As the receiving agent deals with these invoices after the products are checked in, the invoices will need to be entered into the system. Someone in the accounting office usually does this, and oftentimes there is a person whose primary job is dealing with the accounts payable. Once these invoices make their way to the person who enters these, then the actual process of getting the invoices into the system is the next step.

Most software systems have accounts payable modules that are all similar. The system will ask you to enter the vendor, invoice date, and invoice dollar amount. Beyond that, some of the software programs will allow the account code to be a memorized function, and that information will auto-fill if possible. If not or for any invoices that have multiple lines of classification necessary, the person entering the invoices will need to enter the expense code as part of the data that is needed when entering in an invoice.

Most systems also have the capacity to scan in the invoice so an actual copy of the invoice is saved so it can be viewed whenever someone needs to. Having the ability to refer back to an actual invoice is very important, and if the invoices cannot be scanned in to the accounting system and attached to the payable item that is created in the software, then the hard copy of the invoice should be filed and kept as long as needed.

Once invoices are entered in to the accounting system and posted, it is easy to be able to go back through and look at a P&L and see where the invoices have posted their expense in the account lines that the invoices were coded to. It is a good practice to review the income statement after posting invoices. If there are invoices posted to the wrong account code, it can be very obvious that there was some incorrect coding based on where the expenses show up on the P&L.

If it turns out that you have posted something to the wrong account, there are a couple ways that it can be corrected. One way would be to just delete out the invoice and re-enter and repost it, ensuring that it would be going to the correct expense account. Another method to fix an issue like that would be to create a journal entry that reclassifies the expense to the correct location. For example, if you had an expense that was supposed to go to expense line 65000 (R&D food tasting) but was accidentally sent to line 60500 (bar payroll), the correction would be to do a journal entry and credit the given amount to the account line 60500 (bar payroll) and a corresponding debit to 65000 (R&D food tasting), as that will assign the proper expense to the proper location.

When an invoice is entered into the system, it does create a two-sided entry so it is in balance. The debit will show up in the designated expense line; the credit for the same amount will show up in the line that is for accounts payable. In order to make sure that only payable items have made it to that account and nothing has been accidentally booked to that line, if you were to run an aging report (which shows all of the open invoices in the payable system), the total outstanding payable amount on that report should be the exact same amount that would show up on the balance sheet line for accounts payable.

As mentioned previously, entering invoices is just one method of getting your expenses into your accounting system. A second method to bring in expenses is by doing a journal entry for expenses that are incurred that do not have an invoice that needs to be paid. The best example of this would be the payroll process. With most payroll companies, whatever the amount that the total is for the given payroll run is impounded from the designated bank account and will show on a bank statement as just a total dollar amount.

For this exercise, we will say that a given payroll run is $50,000. When you look at your bank statement, you will simply see a line for $50,000 coming out and going to the payroll company. It is your job to make sure that all of the proper account lines show the needed activity. It is fairly common to have the payroll component broken down to reflect FOH labor, BOH labor, management labor, and employee benefits. The employee benefits section includes taxes, 401(k) contributions, workers' comp expenses, employee meals, and anything else included in payroll expenses that are not wages paid for hours of work.

Once you have all of the applicable data from the payroll period, all of the items that comprise the restaurant's payroll (FOH labor, BOH labor, management labor, etc.) should equal what has been impounded. If it does not match, then you will need to see if the wrong amount were impounded or if there was an error in the data that you received that shows the breakdown for each division.

Assuming that the totals match, then you simply need to create a journal entry that reflects the amount that is coming out of the bank as a credit and all of the labor expense lines as a debit. Once this is done, it is a good practice to go back and look at the P&L to make sure the amounts posting to each expense line look correct. If something does not look correct, the easiest way to make that correction would usually be to just make a journal entry to make any needed adjustment. It is very helpful to ensure that you label all of your journal entries very clearly so that if you ever have to go back and look at an old entry, there is no confusion as to what you are looking at.

Outside of the payroll and the physical invoices that get entered into your system, there are also going to be items that occur that will be represented on the bank statement that are automatically pulled from the bank account, for instance, filed taxes, utilities that occur every month, insurance premiums, and anything else that can be set up to be pulled automatically. When these items occur, the expense needs to be entered into the system via a journal entry. In order to properly book these expenses, you would need to debit the proper expense line and credit the cash account. The crediting of the cash account line shows the cash leaving the operating account.

As these entries are made, they will need to be reconciled on a daily basis (if possible) so you are sure that your active cash balance is correct. These expenses will show up on the P&L as soon as they are posted. In the same manner as checking the invoices that were entered into your system, it is always a good idea to review your income statement once you have posted the expenses pulled directly from your operating account to ensure you have posted everything to the correct expense lines.

This covers the majority of the payable items that make up the expenses on your P&L. There will be other expenses that also do need to get recorded to show up on the financial statement on a monthly basis, as these were already paid at a point earlier in the year. This is refers to any prepaid expenses, capital expenses, and items that will need to be amortized or depreciated over a period of time. For capital expenses, these purchases have a life span of more than a year, for example, furniture, fixtures and equipment (FFE), office and computer equipment, and building expenses that raise the value of the building.

When these items are purchased, the expenses do not go to the P&L initially. It will be reflected on the balance sheet. It is booked this way because all of the expense for the purchase does not want to be represented in any one specific month. Instead, this is something that would want to be spread over a longer time frame to be determined.

For example, if you have an insurance bill in the amount of $12,000 that needs to be paid all at once, you would pay that amount, but you would not want to take a $12,000 hit on your P&L in one reporting period since the insurance coverage is for an entire year. Since this would be spread equally at $1,000 per month for an entire year, you would want to code this bill so it would be shown as a prepaid item and then make entries each month to show $1,000 in expenses to general insurance while reducing the prepaid expense line on the balance sheet by the same $1,000 each month. Over the course of one year, that expense is shown in total but spread out so as to not carry too much expense in any one month.

The same types of entries are made when it comes to booking any sort of depreciation that occurs on a monthly basis. Depreciation is used in relation to tangible assets. Depreciation is calculated when you first determine the expected life span of the asset. After that, you would divide the total value of the asset by the number of years in the life of the asset and then multiply by 2 in order to find the depreciation rate. Taking the asset's purchase price, you multiply that amount by the depreciation rate. That is the amount that needs to be booked as an expense each month while reducing the current value by the same amount.[7] This needs to be done each month as depreciation is an ongoing event.

This covers the majority of the items that would show up on your income statement on a monthly basis and how they get brought into the system. In addition to checking your P&L as expenses are added to it in any of the fashions listed above, there will also be the need to check the balance sheet in order to make sure that any of the entries being made for capital expenses, amortizations, or depreciations are being recorded against the proper balance sheet lines in order to reduce those the proper amount.

A good method to use in order to make sure that this is happening is to have a series of sub schedules that reflect the activity

[7] "How to Calculate Depreciation on Fixed Assets", Wikihow.com, March 29, 2019, https://m.wikihow.com/Calculate-Depreciation-on-Fixed-Assets

that is booked each month and make sure there is a month-over-month consistency. By doing that check, you will be able to ensure that everything that needs to be booked as a recurring entry has been done.

Wrapping up this chapter, we focused on the expenses that fill out your P&L and primarily looked at the following areas:

- Expenses are entered into the system via several ways. The most common is to have invoices that are entered and then scanned in, but journal entries exist as well. The entries can be either for items that just need to be posted for singular expenses or memorized, recurring entries that are the same each period.
- It is important to code all of these invoices and entries properly so the expenses are reflected to the proper general ledger line and show the proper expense in the proper area of your P&L.
- Make sure to review your work each day so if any mistakes have been made, they can be corrected as quickly as possible. It is just easier to remember what you may have made a mistake on if you catch it that day as opposed to days further down the line.

CHAPTER 5

The Importance of Inventory Control as It Relates to Restaurant Profitability

We have looked at what makes up the P&L, discussed how the expenses get into the accounting system and show up on the P&L, and talked about tracking the revenues that come in via sales. Now we want to look at how a restaurant can either be profitable or lose money. The simple answer to how a restaurant can be profitable is that it brings in more money than it spends. If it were as easy to do that as I just made it sound, then we would never see any restaurants or bars close. The fact is that even if you have very good revenue, several areas of the restaurant could just be leaking money.

In order for a restaurant to be profitable, there needs to be a focus on both the revenues and the expenses to be able to achieve profitability. The revenue side of the equation is rather easy to track as there is a direct correlation between the number of customers that come to your restaurant, what the average ticket size is, and what the total revenue is. When it comes to the expenses, many different areas need to be monitored to ensure that there is a level of fiscal responsibility being adhered to.

When breaking down expenses, items fall into two categories: controllable and uncontrollable expenses. Whereas uncontrollable expenses are items that the normal flow of business (e.g., property taxes, insurance, and rent) cannot control, controllable expenses are items that an operator has a direct influence over (e.g., payroll, cost of sales, and materials).

Within the realm of the controllable expenses, there are three general areas that the majority of the expenses can be governed. Those are making sure that a proper menu pricing structure is in place, ensuring the controllable expenses are in line with a solid working budget, and making sure there are sound inventory practices in place.

The proper menu pricing will go a long way in making sure that the restaurant's food and beverage cost are within the range that the restaurant has set. For example, if you want to run a 30 percent food cost, an entrée item that costs the house $3 to make needs to be sold at $10 in order to maintain the proper food percentage cost. A balancing act needs to take place. If the entrée is priced too high, you will lose customers due to high prices. If the pricing is too low, the house will lose money. There is the exception of a "loss leader" item on a menu, however. This is a menu item that is designed to be sold at above the set cost price, but it serves the purpose to bring in customers to the restaurant, as revenue is ultimately generated by having customers.

As the restaurant brings in revenue through the course of a period/month, there should be the corresponding invoices being entered as payables that will show the expenses for the same time period. This will allow the operator to watch and see if the controllable expenses are keeping in line with the budget that has been created.

For example, if the budget for linen use for the period is 1 percent and there is $100,000 in sales, then the proper expense for the period for linen would be $1,000. If the total sales for the period is higher than the budget, then more money can be spent on the different expenses. Conversely if the sales are lower than budget, expenses need to be lowered as well.

While most controllable expenses are not inventoried, the restaurant's food and beverage purchases are. This is a critical piece of the process because this will expose bad ordering habits, improper invoice pricing, and waste/theft. The basic principle of an inventory is that more product is retained from the prior reporting period, as well as what is purchased during the current period, than what is used in a given reporting period and that the product that sits on the shelves does not get counted as an expense for the period. Just the opposite, what remains on the shelves works as a credit against the expense. The closing inventory counts for each product/category for a reporting period will then be the opening inventory for those products/categories for the following month. When calculating a food or beverage cost percentage for a period, the formula is taking the opening inventory amount, adding all of the purchases for the period, and subtracting the closing inventory amount for the period. That total is divided by the sales for the same time period.

$$(OI + purchases - CI = x; x/sales = period\ cost)$$

If proper inventory controls are not in place, you will be getting back inaccurate costing percentages and thus either over- or understating your restaurant's financial position.

The first step of doing an inventory is the manual count process. This is done by physically going though and counting each product that is listed on a count sheet, a listing of every single item that can be received through the ordering process. When doing an inventory, it should be done (if possible) by two people, one to count and another to write down the totals. This also largely eliminates the potential for any theft during the inventory process. When writing down the counts, the handwriting needs to be as neat and clean as possible to eliminate any confusion of what the counts are. This is an example of a portion of an inventory count sheet. This is the bread section of the count sheets.

Item	count total
BREAD BAGUETTE	
BREAD BAGUETTE MULTIGRAIN	
BREAD BOULE	
BREAD BRAID	
BREAD BRIOCHE	
BREAD MULTIGRAIN SQ	
BREAD PARKER HOUSE BUNS	
BREAD PUMPERNICKLE	
BREAD SOURDOUGH OBL	
BREAD SOUTHERN SANDWICH	
BREAD MULTIGRAIN SQ	

If it is possible to use a tablet or iPad when doing counts, that is even better so the numbers are clear when it is time to enter the total into the accounting system. When entering the count totals into the system, it is also important to ensure that the data is going in as accurately as possible. Mistakes will inevitably happen, but there are ways to flag those mistakes so they are easily detected and fixed before an inventory is finalized and the costs are set based on faulty data.

After entering the inventory count data into the accounting system, there needs to be a check to ensure that the current data is in line with what the standard count totals are for each product. This can be done by running a report that compares the prior period counts to the current period counts. If there is an existing variance that seems to be above a standard variance percentage, then it would be wise to verify that the entered count was accurate. This could be a matter of a count on the count sheet being incorrect or what is keyed in was done incorrectly.

For example, if there was supposed to be a 10.5 count of a product and 105 was entered by mistake, your inventory, and hence your inventory value, will be misrepresented. Once the counts have been verified for their accuracy, the next step would be to ensure that all of the values are correct.

In checking the values of each item, once again you are looking for a variance in a value from the prior period to the current period that seems to be outside of the normal variance. If you find any items that this would apply to, there are only a couple of reasons as to why this could occur. You have already checked to make sure that the counts that were entered were correctly, so the only factors that could be driving a large change in an item's value would either be that the pack size or the purchase price has changed. Since most accounting systems work with the function that the last invoice entered into the system dictates the price of that item for the period, if an item has the wrong price, it will skew that item's value for the period and change the overall value of the inventory.

In order to check the item pricing, again a report needs to be run that will compare the price variance from the prior to the current period. If there is a variance that would exceed what is considered a normal variance, then there needs to be research into the invoices for the period to see if there were a change in the pricing from the vendor or if there were an error in entering the invoice data.

This could also be due to a change in pack sizing for products. For example, if you order a thirty-pound case of shredded cheese, the pack size was three bags of ten pounds, and the price was $30, your system might recognize that each pack was $10. If the vendor then started carrying the same product but the pack size was six bags at five pounds each, your system may still recognize that each bag was worth $10 and again skewing the overall value of the inventory.

For both food and beverage inventory, you are doing the same procedure, counting items that are not in a prep stage and assigning them a dollar value. While the act of counting is the same for all items, there are some differences as it applies to food and beverage inventory. Generally speaking, most of the inventory for food items are counted in reference to what their unit of measurement is.

For food, this means the unit of measure could be based on an individual count of an each or the pack size, which could be any number of units of measurement, including by pound, ounce, case, gallon, and so on. For beverages, regardless of bottle size, the unit of measure is usually counted as an each. That would mean that if there is a case of beer that needs to be counted, it would not be counted as one case, but twenty-four each. There is a reason why this is done in this manner, for in most accounting systems, beverage is calculated on an each basis.

For example, if you have 380 beers of one type, you would not want to say that you had 15.83 cases of beer, as you are creating extra levels of numeric conversion. It is just easier to say that you have 380 each and then multiply that count of 380 with the value of what one beer would be. Let's say that the value of one beer is $0.95, so the inventory value for this item would be $361. This is also important as it applies to liquor and sometimes wine inventory. For beer, if you sell a bottle of beer, you have sold a whole unit. When you are selling a liquor drink, you are selling only a portion of the bottle, not the whole thing.

With that in mind, when doing the inventory, you would count a partial bottle on a percentage basis. If you have a half a bottle of vodka, you would have a 0.5 count. For a bottle that was three quarters full, it would be a 0.75 count and so on. This can also be applied to bottles of wine that are sold by the glass with the same percentage count system being used. This is one more reason that beverage is most usually counted as an each as opposed to a case.

Case sizes can vary. For beer, most cases are going to be twenty-four beers per case. For wine, it is usually twelve per case. For liquor, cases can be either six or twelve bottles per case. In addition to that, it is possible to buy partial cases of a product of wine and liquor. If you needed eight bottles of vodka, you can order that from your distributor whereas you can't order fourteen individual beers. There is a good chance that you will be charged a split-case fee for ordering a partial case of liquor or wine, as this is a surcharge that some distributors will assign for the work that goes in to opening a case and pulling out what is not wanted so you are receiving just what you ordered. This split-case surcharge gets absorbed into the price of the purchase and ultimately factors into your beverage cost.

By checking all of these functions of your inventory, you can be assured that you are accurately representing the proper value of your goods each period. The inventory function can also serve as a method to know if you are being responsible with purchases. If you are carrying a large inventory month after month, you are tying up money that could be better used elsewhere. By maintaining a bloated inventory, you also run the chance of having items go out of date and having to be thrown out. When that occurs, you are getting zero return on your purchasing dollar, which will ultimately drive up your cost percentages.

By doing a timely and accurate inventory, you give yourself the opportunity to make sure that your stock is being rotated and used in the proper order, thus cutting down on waste and increasing profitability. It is also a good idea to ensure that you track your inventory by category so you can see the trend in value for each category over the course of time. This will help you notice changes in ordering patterns and product pricing as well.

As it applies to controlling the inventory and the money that is tied up with inventory, it is important to work within established par levels as it applies to your ordering. (A Par level – Periodic Automatic Replenishment – or 'safety stock' level is the expected inventory quantity required to be held in reserve to ensure that the customer supply requirements are met.) This is truer with food than it is with beverage, and within the food ordering, certain food items need to be handled differently and with more vigilance than others do. If you are wanting to order up on meats and/or seafood, there is always the option of having these purchased items go into the freezer for longer-term storage.

So if you have the option to make a moneywise purchase in bulk, there is a working window of time that these items can be put to use before they would go bad. For produce, however, there is not the option of freezing these products, so even with refrigeration, there is still only a short life span for these products to be used. With most produce having a storage life of less than one week, it is important to know what is needed as a par level for each produce item so you are ordering enough product to not run out, but not so much as to have product that will go unused. It is also vital to make sure that you are using the oldest product first and properly rotating what is on hand in order to maximize the usage potential of all of your purchases. This is where knowing your par levels relates directly to being fiscally responsible with your ordering.

With the beverage side of the ordering process, there is more flexibility because the storage life for beverage products is considerably longer than that of food product. Beverage products do not need to be stored in a refrigerated area, whereas a majority of food products need to be stored in a refrigerated area. There are also case deals that could be available in the purchasing of beverages that do not exist for food purchases.

For example, you may need to order nine cases of vodka to get to your proper par level, but you find out that if you order a tenth case, the distributor will give you two for free. This changes the price per bottle cost in your favor to a degree that it now becomes in your best interests to order over your par level in order to take advantage of the pricing differential. This can be done because it is easy to store a couple of extra cases of the vodka and use them as needed versus having to occupy your cooler with a product that has a much shorter shelf life.

There is a caveat to this ordering process, however. You need to make sure that you are not overordering and creating a situation where you have dead stock, inventory that does not get moved and has a very low chance of being moved in the future. As opposed to maximizing your purchasing dollar by getting a reduced cost for your beverage purchases through buying in bulk, overordering and having dead stock works directly against that concept as dead stock is only expense with no return revenue.

This goes back to the concept of responsible ordering practices. It is very helpful to know what good inventory ratios are when it comes to ordering. There is a formula figuring out what your inventory ratio is, and this applies to liquor, beer, and wine. Since ordering is done (usually) on a weekly basis, there would need to be an inventory done each week in order to be able know what the weekly usage is. You will need to multiply your beverage cost by your sales to figure out the usage cost.

For example, if you sell $10,000 in bottled beer and you are running a 25 percent cost for bottled beer, your cost for that product was $2,500 for the reporting period. After doing inventory, you will want to divide your current on-hand value by the cost of the product that was sold during that week. For example, if you have $7,500 in bottled beer in your inventory, then you are running at a 3:1 ratio, which is very good. In order to keep a manageable inventory amount of beverage on hand and not tying up money in product that is just sitting on the shelves, a good target to stay below is a 4:1 ratio.[8]

In summation, we covered a good amount of detail on how to handle inventory and what to look for to make sure that your information is correct. To recap:

- Be neat and clean on your count sheets because that data will be entered into your accounting system. It is also possible to make a keying error when entering that data into your system, so the cleaner everything is, the better the chances that you will enter correct data.
- There will be a value for everything that you report inventory amounts on. Keep track of prior period data so you can look back and see if there is a value that looks either too high or low in comparison to the previous period. This will allow you to know quickly if you need to look at the inventory data that made it into your system.
- You learned how to calculate the cost of food and beverage. You arrive at the COGS by taking the opening inventory + purchases for the period − closing inventory = x; x/sales=cost percentage.

---

[8] "Do you have too much liquor inventory on hand?", Blog.bar-i.com. accessed August 8, 2019, https://blog.bar-i.com/do-you-have-too-much -liquor-inventory-on-hand

CHAPTER 6

Proper Menu Pricing to Achieve Desired Food Cost Percentages

Another main area of focus to try to maximize restaurant profitability is ensuring that you are on point when it comes to hitting your assigned food and beverage costs. One of the challenges to this is to verify that you are charging the correct amount for all of the items on the menu. There is a balance that must be maintained so the prices are fair to the customer as well as the restaurant. The managers should be held responsible for maintaining the proper cost percentages that the restaurant sets, but that becomes a very difficult task if the menu pricing does not allow that to happen. A proper food percentage should be at around a 35 percent for a high-end restaurant, and 28 percent is a good percentage for mid-level/fast, casual dining.[9]

For food cost, unlike beverages, multiple variables emerge when trying to achieve a certain cost percentage. These factors, for the most part, can be traced back to what drives the pricing that the vendors set for the products they are selling. There are

---

[9] "4 things to know about your food cost percentage", Upserve.com, December 7, 2018, https://upserve.com/restaurant-insider/4-things-know-food-cost-percentage/

also direct and indirect factors that control how pricing is set. An example of a direct factor would be if there were a particularly long, harsh winter and some of the spring produce that you normally purchase is not as available as it normally would be. Based on supply and demand, this would cause the price to go up for this produce.

An example of an indirect factor would be that the same long, cold winter affected the production of the grain used as feed for the livestock that makes the steaks that your restaurant purchases. Because of the shortage in the grain, the cost of the grain goes up. When the cost of the grain goes up, the cost to the distributor goes up for the production of the beef. When the distributor's costs go up, those increases are passed along to the purchaser so the distributor is still able to meet their budgets. So now the restaurant has to deal with increased costs, and depending on how long the increased costs from the distributor maintains, the restaurant needs to figure out how to keep their costs in line with their desired percentages.

The restaurant can look at a couple of avenues when making their purchases of their products in order to maximize their spending dollar and not have to resort to changing their menu pricing. For instance, this includes buying in greater volume, working with vendors exclusively and locking in set pricing for a determined length of time, finding alternate vendors to supply the product, taking an item off a menu until it becomes economically feasible to carry that product again, and, usually as a last resort, changing the menu pricing.

Buying in volume is a good and easy route to take to get better pricing on items, but especially as it relates to perishable items, there needs to be a vigilance with the use and storage of these products because if proper storage or use is not maintained, then there is greater chance of waste occurring. That is a worst-case scenario as the restaurant gets zero return on its purchasing dollar when there is waste. Setting long-term pricing with a vendor is a good idea if there is a product that is purchased from that vendor exclusively and there is no chance that you want to buy from a different vendor.

The issue with this is that you limit your purchasing flexibility. Finding alternate vendors to supply your restaurant with certain products is always a good idea regardless, but the issue that may occur with this is that the quality of a product provided by one vendor is different than that of another, despite the fact that it is essentially the same product being purchased. Taking an item off the menu can be risky as that may be one of the primary menu items that draws customers to come to the restaurant.

There is a balance that needs to be kept, however, as it is not wise to purchase products that have a limited life span at an inflated price that might not get sold because the price that would be passed along to the guest would also be inflated. This is the case with fresh seafood when something is listed at "market price." Changing a menu price is a last resort. Whereas it might be necessary to make the change in order to keep the costs in line with your desired costing percentage, frequent customers often quickly notice price changes.

The majority of the guests who come to a restaurant do not think about all of the factors that go in to making sure that food and beverage cost percentages are met. They just know that a certain dish was $9.99 last week and $10.99 this week. The key to the purchase of anything is to make sure that the guest feels that they got what they paid for because, as a restaurant guest, they have options to go to your establishment or somewhere else. If they feel that they are being priced out of their comfort range at your establishment, they will go elsewhere.

The cornerstone to making sure that you are meeting your desired food costs is to know what the plate cost of each menu item is. This means that there should be a recipe for each item that can be served to a guest, and from that recipe, the cost of each menu item can be determined. Once that is established, then you will know if the price for the guest is within the proper boundaries to keep your restaurant within the cost percentages that have been budgeted.

In addition to the recipes that should be created and maintained for all of the items that can be served, there also needs to be a set of sub recipes that need to be created to cover the cost of sauces, dressings, garnishments, and so on. For example, if a guest orders a steak with a bourbon reduction sauce, there would need to be a cost for the sauce that is used, in addition to the actual steak cost as well as any additional sides that are served.

In creating the sub recipes, the volume of what is being created needs to be taken into account as the amounts of the ingredients will be in direct proportion to what is being made. Referring back to the bourbon reduction sauce, the ingredients are bourbon, brown sugar, soy sauce, cider vinegar, garlic, and black pepper. Based on how much of the bourbon sauce is being made will then determine how much of these ingredients need to be included.

Let's say that you are wanting to create a half gallon of sauce. With that amount, you know you would need to use four cups of brown sugar. Brown sugar, however, is purchased in ten-pound bags when purchased from the vendor. We know that a pound of packed brown sugar (which is called for in most recipes that use it) is right about two cups. So let's say that the purchased bag of brown sugar costs $10. By that standard, four cups of brown sugar (roughly two pounds) would cost $2.

The same method of expense extrapolation needs to be done for the remaining ingredients that make up a recipe for any sauces or dressings. Once this is completed, then there will be a cost for the sauce being created. Let's say that the half gallon of bourbon reduction sauce being created costs $4 of product to make. On the steak being served, two ounces of sauce is being used. At the cost that was established, the sauce put on the steak would cost the house around $0.13.

This is the basic template that is used in completing total plate costing as it applies to what a guest orders and what it costs the house to create. By knowing what all of the components of an order is and working against what the desired food cost is, the restaurant should be able to then set their menu pricing at the appropriate numbers so they can achieve their desired food costs.

For example, if a guest orders a fourteen-ounce steak with the bourbon reduction sauce and that comes with a baked potato and a side of mixed vegetables, the pricing procedure would work in the same manner as figuring out the cost for the sauce that was created. You would need to figure out the price of each of the vegetables that comprise the side that is served, as well as the potato and steak.

For the potatoes, we will say that those are purchased in a fifty-pound bag. Once the average weight of one potato is established, then it is easy to figure out how much the cost of that one item is from the entire purchase amount. The same would apply to the steak. If the meat is purchased in a larger size and an in-house butcher cuts it down to size, there would be a price that the meat was purchased in per pound. This can quickly be calculated to the price per ounce and thus have a set pricing standard for a cut of meat that was twelve ounces, fourteen ounces, and so on.

Here is an example of what a recipe for this menu item could look like:

menu item: 14 oz. NY Strip				
Item: 14 oz prime cut with sides of mixed veg and baked potato				
recipe unit	quantity	ingredient	unit cost	extended price
ounce	14	NY strip cut of beef	0.5975	8.37
fluid oz	2	bourbon reduction sauce	0.06	0.13
each	1	potato	1	1
single serving	1	mixed vegetables	2.55	2.55
			total cost	12.05
			menu price	43
			gross profit	30.95
			food cost %	28.02%

This is the breakdown of what would make up the components and pricing if someone orders the fourteen-ounce New York strip steak on the menu for their entrée. How this is read is that the unit of measurement is the recipe unit; unit cost is how much one unit costs to purchase.

In this particular case, the cut of meat is listed in the recipe unit of measure as ounces because that is the lowest unit of measure that can be used. By working with the lowest unit of measurement, the quantity will be the size of the cut of meat, so if that number were to change, the math being used will stay constant. Meat, when purchased, is usually purchased by the pound, but when converting to a recipe, it is better to use the lowest level of measurement for building out a recipe. If a pound of beef is $9.56 per pound, you know that it is $0.5975 by the ounce.

So if the menu item is for a fourteen-ounce steak, it is cleaner to have the unit of measure being ounces as opposed to pounds because if you are working with pounds, the quantity would be 0.875 pounds as opposed to 14 ounces. To get to the extended price, it is simply multiplying the unit cost by the quantity. In this case, 0.5975 x 14 = 8.37.[10]

Everything that makes up the plate of food that goes out to

---

[10] "National Retail Report", ams.usda.gov. accessed June 17, 2019, https://www.ams.usda.gov/mnreports/lswbfrtl.pdf

the guest needs to be listed on the recipe as this ultimately will show you what the food cost is for this particular item, so you will know if this plate of food will be above, at, or below your target food cost.

For recipe items comprised of multiple parts, there also will exist sub recipes. In the case of the fourteen-ounce New York strip steak, two items make up that plate cost that would have sub recipes. The reduction sauce that goes on the steak is made in volume. (We said we made a half a gallon.) There would also be a recipe for the mixed vegetables, as these are comprised of separate items that are combined to make one whole menu item. The process to build out the sub recipes is exactly the same as you take the ingredients and figure out what the cost is to build out what would be considered a whole production item.

Again, for the reduction sauce, we made a half gallon, but we are going to call a unit of measure an ounce as you are only going to use an ounce or two for each served steak. For the potatoes, if we know that these are purchased in large bags, you would figure out the number of potatoes that make up the weight total and then divide that by the cost to give a cost total.

For this exercise, we said that one potato costs $1. The same methodology would work for the mixed vegetables as you would calculate what the total purchase amount would be for each item in mix and then reduce that to the amount that is the serving portion. For this exercise, we will say that it is a six-ounce portion of mixed vegetables that consists of green beans, corn, carrots, and peas. You would figure out what the lowest unit of measurement is that you are going to use and build your recipe around that. In this case, again it would be ounces, and your sub recipe for the mixed vegetables would look something like this:

menu item: mixed vegetables				
recipe unit	quantity	ingredient	unit cost	extended price
ounce	1.5	carrots	0.5	0.75
ounce	1.5	peas	0.75	1.13
ounce	1.5	corn	0.25	0.37
ounce	1.5	green beans	0.2	0.3
			total cost	2.55

The total cost is the cost for one serving of the vegetable for every plate that gets them as a side item. You are not including the menu price, gross profit, or food cost percentage in this, as this is an item that is part of a bigger whole. So the price is absorbed in the plate cost of the steak. Since the plate cost of this entrée is at 28.02 percent, you have priced this at or below your breakeven point, so this is a profitable entrée item on your menu. All of the parts that make this up are priced properly in your menus and sub menus.

The good thing is that the majority of the restaurant accounting programs have built-in modules that create the plate pricing for menu items based on the purchasing that is entered into the program through the accounts payable/invoice entry process. (See chapter 4 if you forgot how that process works.) The way that this would work is that as invoices are entered into the system for payment, the program will pull the most recent pricing information in as the recognized price. Then that will allow the system to include the proper costing for recipes.

For example, if you were pricing out the cost to make a pizza, you would have all of the ingredients that make up the dough as a sub recipe, and the dough would be the recipe item. The same concept would maintain for the pizza sauce and any spices included in the sauce. Then you would have the cheese and any additional toppings. For simplicity reasons, we will focus on the cheese and how that would work in the system. The cheese, when purchased, is purchased in a thirty-pound case. Let's just say that it is $30 for the case of cheese, making it $1 per pound, or $0.0625 per ounce.

If your software has the module to be able to build out recipes, then all you would need to do would be to list the products used in the recipe and the amount. In this case, as it applies to the pizza, the dough would already have its cost, as that was created in the sub recipe and likewise the sauce. So when you get to the cheese, you would enter in the type of cheese (e.g., mozzarella) and the amount being used. For this exercise, we will say that eight ounces are used.

If your purchasing items are set up properly, there will be a designation of what a proper measurement size is for recipe purposes. In this case, the designation would be by the ounce. This way when you enter the recipe and you list eight ounces of the cheese, the system knows what the case price is, and thus what the ounce price is, so your recipe would list the cost of the cheese used as $0.50 for that pizza.

If the software you use does not have a recipe built-out module, this information can still be built out by hand by using Excel (or a similar program). The starting point would be whatever the purchase size is of any product and then being able to take that pricing and move that to whatever the recipe dictates. The example listed above regarding the cheese is a good example of purchase price of an item versus the usage amounts. Once you have established what the price is per a standard unit of measurement, whether it is a pound, ounce, or something smaller, it becomes easy to arrive at that extended cost based on how much of the product is being used.

Once you have figured out how much everything on the menu costs the house to purchase, the prices on the menu can be set with relative ease, as there will be a direct correlation between the two. There will be some items on any menu that will exceed what you would like to have as your food cost. (Again, this would be commonly seen with seafood that is listed at market cost.) But if done properly, there will be plenty of items on your menu that will allow you to make up ground. Some of the items that allow for a larger markup are as follows:

- Fountain drinks and coffee: Each of these costs the restaurant less than $0.25, and they can be priced at $2 or higher. Even with free refills, this is a moneymaking product.
- Pizza: Including the dough, cheese, and toppings, most pizzas would cost around $5 or less to make and can be sold for over twice that amount.
- Soups: Since you can use the trimmings from other items (meats and vegetables) to create stock, you can produce a large volume of a soup at a low cost and sell it at a premium price by the bowl. This allows you to cut down on waste and maximize your purchasing dollar.
- Breakfast items: If you are lucky enough to serve breakfast, there are potentially big margins to be found in the sale of any breakfast foods. These require low amounts of prep work and labor, and all of the ingredients are relatively cheap for most breakfast foods.

It is important to have a good balance between the sale of these items so you can stay within your set margins. This is where it is helpful for your service staff to have a thorough working knowledge of your menu and the costs related to each of the menu items. If a guest has questions regarding the menu and what they would like to order, in addition to having the opportunity to upsell the guest right away, the server also has the opportunity to try to guide the guest to selecting a menu item that will maximize the restaurant's food cost. We are, after all, trying to be a profitable enterprise.

Since we are trying to achieve maximum profitability with your restaurant, we covered a number of pertinent points in this chapter. Those were:

- What are some of the different purchasing options that will help you maximize your purchasing dollar?
- How do you build out the recipes and sub recipes for all of the menu items and figure out what the cost of each menu item is? By having this information, proper plate costing can be achieved so you can make sure that you are able to meet your set food costs.
- What are some examples of food items that are able to stay below your budgeted food costs and help keep your costs low?

CHAPTER 7

Proper Menu Pricing to Achieve Desired Beverage Cost Percentages

In the same manner as trying to maintain a food cost that will allow for profitability, there are cost percentage targets for your beverage costs. Since your beverage is ordered and sold separately as liquor, beer, and wine, there are individual revenue lines on your P&L to reflect the sales for each of the three beverage categories. Within the beer cost, there are both bottled beer and draft beer cost, but those are almost always combined as one cost. Good target percentages for each of the categories are as follows:

- Liquor: 17 to 19 percent
- Wine: 27 to 30 percent
- Beer: 21 to 25 percent[11][12]

[11] "Managing the Big Three", Nightclub.com, August 5, 2009, https://www.nightclub.com/operations/managing-big-three

[12] "Rules of Thumb for Beverage Costs: How's your restaurant doing?", Meritagepos.com, accessed June 3, 2019, http://meritagepos.com/rules-of-thumb-for-beverage-costs-hows-your-restaurant-doing/

From these numbers, you can come up with what is referred
to as a blended cost, which is all three categories as one cumulative percentage. Based on what style of establishment you are
dealing with, there can be a big difference in what is driving
your cost depending on if you sell a heavy majority of one type
of beverage over the others. A good target to have as a blended
beverage cost would be 23 percent or lower.

For beverage cost, it is much easier to set the cost percentage
desired and achieve those percentages as there are less variables
to work with. For example, if a case of beer costs the house $24
from the distributor, then each beer costs $1 to purchase. To run
a 25 percent bottled beer cost, the price that would need to be
charged per beer is $4. This should be an easy process to follow
as there is little spillage or waste when it applies to bottled beer.
There is the chance of breakage occurring, but that needs to be
built into the cost percentage ratio.

Because there is breakage, beers that have gone out of date,
or any other reason why a beer may be sent back, the lowest price
that you would want to charge for that beer would be $4.50 as
opposed to $4.00 (which would equate to the exact 25 percent
bottled beer cost). This allows a bit of flexibility for any absorbed
cost that does occur as well as being able to cover the differential
for any "free" beers that may be given out. Obviously, if you want
to try to get your beer cost lower, you raise the price accordingly.
If you were to charge $5 for the same beer, you would be running
closer to a 20 percent bottled beer cost.

In working with liquor, pricing should be affixed to the cost
of a bottle of product as well as the size of the pour being done.
For example, if a customer would like a single liquor drink, like
a gin and tonic, the pricing needs to be centered around the cost
of the bottle of gin. Let's say that the bottle of gin is a $20 bottle.
In making the drink, the amount of gin used is a one-and-a-half-
ounce pour. Keeping in a consistent mix, at a 3:1 ratio of tonic to

gin, there should be about 4.5 ounces of tonic water used. In a 750-milliliter bottle of gin, you could get just under seventeen one-and-a-half ounce pours in making drinks. That would mean that the liquor used in that drink would cost the house $1.18. If the house were working at a 20 percent liquor cost, then this drink should be priced at $6 minimum to cover the cost of the liquor. There are the other costs involved in this drink (the tonic water and the lime garnish), so a reasonable price would be $6.50. This type of breakdown maintains for all liquor drinks as there is a recipe for all drinks, and if everything is priced out to work with the established liquor cost percentage, the pricing of the drinks will adhere to the set beverage cost.

For wine costs, this works in the same manner as liquor, working on the platform that there are six glasses of wine per bottle. The cost percentage that should be a target for wine is 30 percent or lower. The main difference as it applies to wine sales is that the price of wine from the distributor will vary greatly based on type, availability, perceived value, and transport expense, just to name a few factors. So if a bottle of wine were to cost the distributor $10 per bottle, that would be sold to a restaurant for around $20. Keeping with the desired cost percentage, that bottle would be sold in the restaurant to the customer for around $60 to $65.

The final area of beverage expense is for draft beer. This has the largest margin for variance of all of the beverage categories. First off, a good percentage for draft beer cost should be around 22 percent. Some of the factors that come in to play with draft beer, as opposed to the other beverage categories, are spillage, waste (foamy beer, wrong temperature, and dirty draft lines), beverage size, and import versus domestic. A standard half-barrel keg (15.5 gallons) holds 1,984 ounces of beer. From that, if the standard pour is a twelve-ounce beer, the keg holds 165 beers. If it is a sixteen-ounce pour, there are 124 beers per keg. Working with the twelve-ounce pour standard, if a keg cost $100, then each draft beer would cost the house about $0.61. The proper sales price for that beer should then be in the $2.75 to $3.00 range.

The issue that exists with draft beer cost versus the other beverage categories is the ability to monitor and count the product on hand and compare the inventory counts to the daily sales totals. Since there should be a direct correlation among the starting count number of an item and the ending count, the difference should be the number sold, and that would be reflected on a daily sales report to show the number of an item that was sold.

For example, if you started a shift with 150 Bud Lights and ended with 70, the end-of-day sales report should show 80 sold. If the number sold is less than that, this would indicate that there were some of the Bud Lights given away without being rung in. With keg beer, it is very difficult to know how many have been sold during a shift since there is not a specific count that can be done. This allows for the bartenders and servers to give away draft beer easier than any other product without the house being able to prove what was actually sold.

Most establishments actually do have an allowance for some giveaways to loyal customers, promotional reasons, or as an act of good faith. (If someone's food is taking too long in the kitchen to be made, the guest might receive a "free" beer.) However, these do need to be recorded and entered through the POS system so they can be tracked. These will be reflected in a P&L, but because the item was not sold, there would be no revenue to help keep the beverage cost in line. By having these entered through the POS system, the product is tracked so the inventory will make more sense and won't appear as though theft were taking place.

To illustrate that point, if you started with 1,000 beers and sold 700 in the time in between your inventories, you should expect to have 300 remaining. If, when you do inventory, you only count 250, then it looks like 50 beers were either just given away or two cases of beer were stolen. By entering those as comps or on a manager giveaway tab, those are recorded through the system so it makes sense during your inventory as you will now see that there were 750 beers sold (keeping in mind that a comp is really just the house paying for the beer as opposed to the customer).

Since the house is technically paying for comped items, to keep the relationship between sales and COGS correct, you would need to deduct the cost of the comps from the COGS and place the expense in a designated location. After that, you will need to eliminate the retail value of the comps from the sales and expense. Here is how that would be done:

- Initially, comps are recorded at retail value in the appropriate sales category (food or beverage), and the offset for payment not received is temporarily placed in an expense (marketing) account.
- The retail values of the comps for the period are then multiplied by the appropriate cost percentages (food comps x food cost of sales percentage; beverage comps x beverage cost of sales percentage). The results are the costs of food and beverage comps, respectively.
- A journal entry is made to reverse the retail value of comps from the sales and expense accounts. A second journal entry is made to record the cost of comps as a marketing expense and reduce cost of sales by the same amounts.[13]

Here is an example of how this would look. We are going to say that on a given day, $700 in food and $300 in beverage was given away as comped items. Assuming that all of these items

---

[13] "Comps", RestaurantBusinessOnline.com, August 22, 2002, https://www.restaurantbusinessonline.com/comps

were rung through the POS system, at the end of that day, those comps will show in the system as such:

	debit	credit
food sales		700
beverage sales		300
marketing	1000	

This would be part of the DSR information and just embedded in the other numbers that make up the day's total sales information.

We are going to say that the food cost percentage is 30 percent and the beverage cost percentage is 22 percent. So at those percentages, this is what we would come up with for the cost to the restaurant for the food and beverages that were comped for that day:

	percentage	amount	total
food cost %	30.00%	700	210
beverage cost %	22.00%	300	66

Since what you are giving away as a comp is only being given away at cost, you are going to want to reverse the amounts that were part of the day's sales (above), as that is what the sales would be if the products were actually sold. The entry would look like this:

	debit	credit
food sales	700	
beverage sales	300	
marketing		1000

And you would want to enter the value of the product that was given away based on what it actually cost the restaurant, which would look like the following:

	debit	credit
food sales	210	
beverage sales	66	
marketing		276

This also becomes an issue for taxation purposes as there are sales and use taxes as well as separate beverage surtaxes in certain states that the house is essentially absorbing when they comp liquor drinks. The taxes due are based on the sales, and if the house is "paying" for the drinks, then they are also responsible for the tax due. Since there is no money collected on a comped item, there is also no tax amount being paid to the restaurant. When it comes time to pay the taxes, the amount the house is paying for their comped items is coming out of the generated profits.

By following these basic elements for control of beverage pricing, your restaurant should be able to work within your set beverage percentages, and you should be able to arrive at a profitable venture. Like in the previous chapter about food pricing, the goal for the beverage pricing is to maximize the return potential and make your restaurant profitable.

Some of the key points that we looked at were:

- What are the ideal cost percentages for liquor, beer, and wine, respectively, as well as the blended cost percentage for all beverage?
- How, by following recipes, do you know how to figure out the cost of what any drink would cost to make? And how do you properly price that drink so it falls within the

proper cost percentage and works as a moneymaker for the restaurant?

- Why is it important to track drinks that are given away as "free" for proper inventory tracking and also tax implications?

CHAPTER 8

Restaurant Compliance and Hidden Expenses

At any restaurant or bar, there are rules and regulations on how processes and procedures need to be handled. All of these should be in print and kept somewhere handy so they can be referred to whenever needed. They should also be summarized in the employee handbooks that should be given to each new hire when they start with the company. The rules, regulations, processes, and procedures are referred to as compliance items.

The word *compliance* carries a certain gravitas as it applies to the restaurant industry. There are the legal iterations for the term. For instance, did the monthly taxes get filed on time so your restaurant is in compliance with the tax laws? There is the operations concept of the term. For example, are the food coolers at the proper temperature so food is being prepared in a safe manner? Then there is the more internal use of term, and this would be more geared toward if the employees are following the rules that are set for the operation of the restaurant. We will focus on the latter two areas as it applies to compliance and how it affects the expenses that the restaurant incurs.

These two areas are facets of the general operations of the restaurant that, on a day-to-day as well as month-to-month level, can have a significant impact on where money is spent and if it is necessary to incur these expenses. As we break down several examples of where the expenses can add up quickly, you will see a difference between the direct and indirect expenses that are a result of the initial problem that incurred the original expense. As is usually the case, if the initial issue is dealt with before it becomes a problem, the more indirect issues and expenses do not ever get a chance to exist.

One of, if not the, primary areas that needs constant vigilance is in the areas of repair and maintenance. If there are parts of the building that need to be brought up to code either internally or externally, these types of issues need to be dealt with immediately, or the restaurant could be shut down due to lack of compliance for building codes. This is the extreme end of not being in compliance. More of the repair and maintenance items have to do with just getting things fixed before they turn into bigger problems.

This is where the hidden expense component can really come in to play. For this exercise, let's say that there is a walk-in cooler that is not staying at its proper temperature. The first step that needs to be taken is to determine why this is happening. Is this a recurring problem, or is this something that is happening for the first time? Hopefully the restaurant is keeping a repair and maintenance log so you can look back and see if the problem you are experiencing is an issue that has been addressed before. This can make a big difference in the cost of what would need to be done in order to get this cooler back up and running. If it is something as simple as a stopped motor needing to be repaired and this was the first time that had ever happened, then this would be a simple repair that would be made, and the cooler would be back up and running.

Conversely, if this is a repeating problem or just another problem in a long line of issues with this equipment, then other steps would need to be taken. First, do a valuation of the cost, where we would start getting into the direct and indirect costs of a repair. Find out how much it cost to have the cooler installed and what the current value of the piece of equipment would be based on the depreciation rate and how long it has been in use.

After that number has been arrived at, you next need to know how much has been paid for any previous repairs and any more repairs that are going to be expected in the near future. Any future repair expense is purely speculative, but the people doing current repairs would be able to let you know if they expect more repairs in the near future. So all of that information will go in to determining what the direct cost of repairing a cooler would be.

But that is only part of the data needed for being able to do a valuation to figure out if it is better to repair or replace this piece of equipment. The indirect cost comes from what is in the cooler. Depending on how long the cooler has not been functioning at the correct level, this will determine what has happened to all of the product inside the cooler.

If the food inside of the cooler has crossed the line for what is considered a safe storage temperature, then all of the product will have to be thrown out. This would be an indirect cost because the food has spoiled due to the storage device not being able to do its job properly, not the fault of the food itself getting old. This is also going to affect the purchase of other product, as there will need to be other cooler space made available to store food while the cooler is repaired.

To extend this concept even further, if you are now dealing with a smaller amount of cooler space, this could affect the size of the orders that you place for perishable goods. If you have set pricing based on orders being a certain size or dollar amount, then you may get charged more for having to make smaller orders. That would get added to the cost total of the repair. The sum of all of those costs need to be weighed against what it would cost to replace the cooler itself.

Where this becomes a restaurant compliance issue is if there is a check and balance in place to make sure that all of the equipment is working in the manner it is supposed to. If and when something goes wrong, there is a system in place on how to proceed. If the rules and standards that are set internally within the restaurant are followed, then potential issues can be addressed at their earliest notice, which will allow the restaurant to move forward with any sort of resolution as quickly as possible. By moving forward quickly on the problem resolution, that will increase the probability that you will be able to minimize the long-term expense that could be incurred.

A second area where compliance can have a profound monetary effect is in product ordering. Whether it is ordering food, beverage, or durable goods, certain standards should be adhered to when placing orders. For the durable goods, what should be considered is making sure that par levels are maintained so that ordering only needs to be done when restocking to a given par level.

By following this process, orders can be done in more of a bulk size, and that will translate into savings as it applies to shipping. For objects like china, glass, and silverware, inventories need to be done regularly to make sure that orders are placed as required but placed in a manner that will maximize the efficiency of what is spent.

When it comes to ordering food and beverage, it takes a bit more diligence to ensure that ordering is done in the most efficient manner to maximize return on the purchasing dollar as well as making sure to have ordered enough product to cover all of the restaurant needs, but not too much so that there is the potential for waste. Depending on your restaurant's relationship with their food and beverage vendors, there is always the potential for pricing deals to be worked out. It is usually easier to get deals as it applies to beverage than food, but several food vendors have the ability to lock in set pricing and get the best payment terms if there are monthly minimums that are hit in regards to the amounts that are ordered.

These types of deals would vary from vendor to vendor, but it is important to ask what is available. Oftentimes, the vendor will ask that you do a certain percentage of your ordering through them in order to get these purchasing deals. If you have a strong selection of vendors to choose from, this is not a bad idea to put in place, as the savings can be substantial over a year's time.

The key to this process is to have a good handle on your ordering needs and par levels. There has to be a balance between what needs to be ordered so the best pricing deals can be achieved without overordering that would have you carrying a bloated inventory or having perishable items go to waste. This requires the person who takes care of the ordering to have a good working knowledge of what needs to be on hand each week in order to cover all of the restaurant activity. This can usually be figured out by referring to prior sales data from previous years.

If there is a consistent pattern shown of what sales are at a particular time of the calendar year, then based on what your food cost would be, you should be able to accurately order what you need without overdoing it. Granted, if you need to make multiple orders in a week from certain vendors, that is not a problem, but the majority of vendors do charge a transport fee, and proper ordering would eliminate an excess of those fees.

Since this is about the hidden costs associated when compliance issues are not met, a large area of hidden cost that is not talked about much is when the restaurant has to absorb the cost of an improperly prepared meal. This can result in an escalated number of comps that have to be done in order to keep a guest happy because they had a meal that was not just unsatisfactory, but one that could cause them to become ill.

In addition to the comps that could be incurred, which have

a direct relation to the bottom line of your P&L, there is also the chance that a guest who had a meal that did not go well could take to social media and post negative comments about the restaurant. This could ultimately result in others reading these comments and deciding to dine at another establishment, thus driving down the potential revenue for your restaurant.

While there is a segment of the dining population that will always find something wrong with their dining experience, the majority of complaints are directly related to the food itself as opposed to the provided service. It is helpful if the guest articulates their concerns during their time in the restaurant so there is a chance that any issues can be resolved. Whereas the finished product that the guest is presented may have some issues (food is cold, meat not cooked to proper temperature, etc.), those are specifics that the guest notices at the time they are dining. It is the oversights that the guests do not notice that can cause some of the bigger problems.

That presents the area of restaurant compliance that has to do with the food handling procedures. This is not just an internal restaurant set of rules. Proper food handling procedures are the law. If proper food handling procedures are not followed, there is a very good chance that there could be cross-contamination, which could lead to foodborne illness. You can't see, smell, or taste harmful bacteria that may cause illness. In every step of food preparation, follow the four steps of the Food Safe Families campaign to keep food safe:

- Clean: Wash hands and surfaces often.
- Separate: Don't cross-contaminate.

- Cook: Cook to the right temperature.
- Chill: Refrigerate promptly.[14]

The storage guidelines for food are very specific. They need to be followed, or the food will need to be thrown out, as once food is outside of the proper storage parameters, it is considered to be unsafe for consumption. If food has to be thrown out, then you will incur an increase in your food cost percentages. Whatever amount was spent in purchasing will obviously return zero revenue. Here are some of the basic food storage rules that need to be followed:

- Always refrigerate perishable food within two hours (or one hour when the temperature is above 90 degrees Fahrenheit [32.2 degrees Celsius]).
- Check the temperature of your refrigerator and freezer with an appliance thermometer. The refrigerator should be at 40 degrees Fahrenheit (4.4 degrees Celsius) or below and the freezer at 0 degrees Fahrenheit (-17.7 degrees Celsius) or below.
- Cook or freeze fresh poultry, fish, ground meats, and variety meats within two days and other beef, veal, lamb, or pork within three to five days.
- Wrap perishable food, such as meat and poultry, securely to maintain quality and to prevent meat juices from getting onto other food.
- To maintain quality when freezing meat and poultry in its original package, wrap the package again with foil or plastic wrap that is recommended for the freezer.

---

[14] "Basics for Handling Food Safely", fsis.usda.gov, accessed July 9, 2019, https://www.fsis.usda.gov/wps/portal/fsis/topics/food-safety-education/get-answers/food-safety-fact-sheets/safe-food-handling/basics-for-handling-food-safely/ct_index

Canned foods are safe indefinitely as long as they are not ex-
posed to freezing temperatures or temperatures above 90 degrees
Fahrenheit. If the cans look ok, they are safe to use. Discard cans
that are dented, rusted, or swollen. High-acid canned food (toma-
toes and fruits) will keep their best quality for twelve to eighteen
months; low-acid canned food (meats and vegetables) will keep
for two to five years.

Just like food storage, the food preparation safety parameters
that need to be followed are critical to make sure that the guests
are not eating food that could lead to illness. The following are
some of the more important rules that need to be followed as it
relates to the sanitation of the employee and the food preparation
area in order to keep foodborne illness potential as low as possible:

- Always wash hands with warm water and soap for twenty
  seconds before and after handling food.
- Don't cross-contaminate. Keep raw meat, poultry, fish,
  and their juices away from other food. After cutting raw
  meats, wash cutting board, utensils, and countertops with
  hot, soapy water.
- Sanitize cutting boards, utensils, and countertops using
  a solution of one tablespoon of unscented, liquid chlorine
  bleach in one gallon of water.
- Marinate meat and poultry in a covered dish in the
  refrigerator.

For storage purposes, a lot of food can be frozen and kept for
a longer period of time than if it were just stored in a cooler. By
freezing food, any microbes that might be present in that food will
become inactive. Once thawed, the microbes can become active
again under the right circumstances, so that is why it is important
to properly cook the food once it has thawed.

Most foods can be frozen, but there are some exceptions,

like eggs in a shell or canned foods. There is always the matter of quality for food that is frozen as well. Raw meat and poultry will maintain their quality, but items such as mayonnaise, lettuce, and cream sauce just do not freeze well. The following are three methods for properly thawing frozen product:

- **Refrigerator:** The refrigerator allows slow, safe thawing. Make sure thawing meat and poultry juices do not drip onto other food.
- **Cold water:** For faster thawing, place food in a leakproof plastic bag. Submerge in cold tap water. Change the water every thirty minutes. Cook immediately after thawing.
- **Microwave:** Cook meat and poultry immediately after microwave thawing.

As it applies to the actual cooking of food, very specific temperatures need to be followed when preparing dishes. This, again, is to make sure that the food being prepared is safe for the guests to consume. Following are the temperatures that need to be met for the cooking of meats:

- Cook all raw beef, pork, lamb and veal steaks, chops, and roasts to a minimum internal temperature of 145 degrees Fahrenheit (62.8 degrees Celsius) as measured with a food thermometer before removing meat from the heat source. For safety and quality, allow meat to rest for at least three minutes before carving or consuming. For reasons of personal preference, consumers may choose to cook meat to higher temperatures.

- Cook all raw ground beef, pork, lamb, and veal to an internal temperature of 160 degrees Fahrenheit (71.1 degrees Celsius), as measured with a food thermometer.
- Cook all poultry to an internal temperature of 165 degrees Fahrenheit (73.9 degrees Celsius), as measured with a food thermometer.

After the food for the guests is cooked, it then needs to be taken out to them. This needs to be done in a timely manner as the food prepared will not keep its integrity if it is kept under a heat lamp for an excessive amount of time (for hot foods) or left at room temperature (for cold foods). The following is a list of what temperatures food should be kept at while it is waiting to be presented to guests:

- Hot food should be held at 140 degrees Fahrenheit (60 degrees Celsius) or warmer.
- Cold food should be held at 40 degrees Fahrenheit (4.4 degrees Celsius) or colder.
- When serving food at a buffet, keep food hot with chafing dishes, slow cookers, and warming trays. Keep food cold by nesting dishes in bowls of ice or use small serving trays and replace them often.
- Do not leave out perishable food for more than two hours at room temperature (or one hour when the temperature is above 90 degrees Fahrenheit [32.2 degrees Celsius]).[15]

By following these food handling guidelines, you will reduce the amount of foods that you have to worry about discarding and

---

[15] "Food Safety Information", fsis.usda.gov, accessed July 9, 2019, https://www.fsis.usda.gov/wps/wcm/connect/18cece94-747b-44ca-874f-32d69fff1f7d/Basics_for_Safe_Food_Handling.pdf?MOD=AJPERES

thus be able to increase your profit margins. The US Department of Agriculture has extensive information available that will list storage temperatures for all types of food as well as more detailed instructions for food handling of varieties. Again, by following these standards, you will keep yourself within the compliance models that your restaurant should maintain, as these are the compliance requirements by law for proper for food service.

The economic impact that could be incurred by not following these regulations can be extremely severe. These are the types of items that are included when a health inspection is done. If these requirements are not met, it could lead to a failing grade, which is the type of action that can cause a restaurant to have to suspend operations until brought up to code or even close the restaurant down.

For the bar/beverage service side of the restaurant, several compliance points need to be followed, and these are very different from the food handling/preparation requirements. There is more margin when it comes to the beverage than food as it applies to the storage. For example, when storing beer, it should be kept in a storage area that is no higher than 55 degrees Fahrenheit (12.8 degrees Celsius) and no lower than 30 degrees Fahrenheit (-1.1 degrees Celsius), although storing below freezing is not optimal for drinking. For wine, the range for storage should be between 45 and 65 degrees Fahrenheit (7.2 to 18.3 degrees Celsius), with 55 degrees Fahrenheit (12.8 degrees Celsius) being considered close to the perfect temperature.

Certain wines do have more specific storage instructions based on their vintage, but those are the minority. For long-term storage, it is always best to keep bottles out of the sunlight as UV rays can damage wine. The proper storage for liquor is to keep bottles in the 60 to 65 degrees Fahrenheit (15.6 to 18.3 degrees Celsius) range, but some liquors can be stored at much colder temperatures. Vodka, for example, can be stored in a freezer.

The real areas of compliance and proper handling procedures for beverages have to do more with the creation and presentation of making drinks and the cleanliness and sanitary conditions of the bar. Three categories of tasks need to be done in order to keep the bar area in the proper shape so it will pass any sort of health inspection: the cleaning that needs to be done throughout the course of a shift, end-of-the-shift tasks, and the cleaning that needs to be performed on a weekly basis.

By doing these tasks on the proper schedule, the cleanliness of the bar will stay where it needs to be, and you will cut down on the issues that could cause any sort of sickness. During the shift, there should be a regular rotation of the following: wiping down the bar, taking out the trash as needed, and cleaning all used glassware.

By completing these items as needed, you will be able to keep your bar clean and stocked with the proper glassware. At the end of the shift, there is a more thorough list of what needs to be done to shut the bar down. Depending on your particular bar and its setup, there may be more that needs to be done, but by doing the following, you will at least be doing the basics to keep your bar within the compliance level of how a bar should be taken care of. These tasks include the following: sweeping up behind the bar, emptying and cleaning the ice bins, cleaning the soda gun (if there is one), taking the bottles out of the speed well and wiping them down, cleaning out the speed well and wiping that down, running the floor mats through the wash, cleaning out and disposing of any garnish that has not been used and cleaning garnish trays, and restocking any sort of bar items as needed (glassware and paper goods).

On a weekly basis, there would need to be a more complete cleaning that takes place. By doing a weekly cleaning, this will cut down on bug, insect, and rodent problems. The weekly cleaning tasks should include the following: cleaning out the reach in coolers; cleaning behind and moveable equipment, including coolers, POS systems, and any other fixtures that are able to be moved; and cleaning all of the areas where glassware is stored and washing the glassware if the area that is being cleaned is dirty.

The list should also include cleaning the keg lines. This might be something that your beverage distributors do for you. If so, make sure that this is done on a regular rotation. Finally ensure that proper pest control measures are taken. Bugs love the sugars that can be present in liquor, and if left unchecked, this can become a big cleanup issue quickly.[16]

The main focus of these tasks is to keep a clean bar area so that in the event of an inspection, the bar area will receive a passing grade. From both a reputation and legal perspective, it is important that the bar maintains the standards that the Department of Health sets in order to be an attractive location to have guests come and dine and drink.

From an internal compliance perspective, there will be rules about how drinks are prepared and presented to the guests. These are important to follow so there is a sense of consistency, regardless of who is working. One of the main areas of focus for a guest is that their drink of choice tastes the same each time they receive one. If there is variation in how a Manhattan is made depending on who the bartender is, there is a chance that the guest will ask for a drink to be remade. When that happens, the proper procedure should be that the drink being remade is still rung in through the POS system so the alcohol being used is tracked. Then the drink that has been replaced should be comped

---

[16] "Back Bar Cleaning Checklist: Everything you need to know to stay up-to-code", Perlick.com, accessed July 14, 2019, https://www.perlick.com/commercial/resources/use-and-care/back-bar-cleaning-checklist/

off. This will allow a proper representation of your beverage cost to be reflected, but this comped item will have an impact on the bottom line of the P&L. (We covered that accounting process in the previous chapter.)

There is no way to list all of the hidden costs that can be incurred at any restaurant or bar because each location is unique unto itself and has a separate set of problems that could arise that are different from any other location. By following all of the compliance guidelines that are in place, you will reduce your risks of having these unforeseen and hidden costs be an issue because you will have prepared for them as best you can. Just being prepared is not enough, however, as there does need to be proper follow-through by the employees and proper supervision by the managers to make sure the compliance standards are being met. Even after doing all of this, there is always going to be the chance that something will break or fail and need immediate attention. By having a plan in place on how to handle these incidents, you will be able to move forward and hopefully only have a minimal impact on your expenses.

The compliance topic covers a lot of different concepts, and we focused on both some internal and external items that are all part of restaurant compliance. The areas we targeted the most were:

- How do we keep track of repair and maintenance issues? Make sure that the restaurant keeps a log to track repairs that are done as well those that need to be addressed. There is also the need for proper valuation tracking to be kept in order to know how much any repair can cost in relation to replacing equipment as needed.
- What do we need to look at for proper product ordering so par levels are maintained for durable goods while trying to maximize your purchasing dollar?

- What are food and beverage handling and storage regulations? How does not being in compliance with these regulations create excess costs for the restaurant that adhering to the outlined standards could have avoided?

CHAPTER 9

Theft and Cash Management in Your Restaurant

Part of always knowing how your restaurant is doing financially is to have a firm grasp on loss prevention. One of the things that is synonymous with a restaurant is theft. Theft can take on all sorts of forms, but regardless of how it is done, if there is any sort of transaction that somehow takes from the profitability of the restaurant and benefits someone else, it is theft. Statistics show that 75 percent of all employees have admitted to stealing from their employer.[17] This adds up to literally billions of dollars per year in industry theft. Theft can take on all sorts of forms in the restaurant, from actually taking product from the restaurant as your own to giving away "free" food or drink or employees actually pocketing cash or shorting the house what is actually due to them.

The purest form of theft happens with employees literally taking product from the restaurant for their own personal use. This issue affects the beverage side of the operation more so than

---

[17] "Employee Theft: Why do employees Steal?", calrest.org, accessed August 8, 2019, https://www.calrest.org/labor-employment/employee-theft-why-do-employees-steal

food due to the packaging that is used for beverages. The simple truth is that it is easier to hide a bottle of liquor that someone will later take home than it would be to try to get a package of ground beef out of the building. It is also a matter of accessibility to the product being stolen that dictates what is being taken.

Usually the beverage storeroom is located someplace where there are not a lot of employees, so if someone has access to this area, the opportunity is there for this person to help themselves to "free" product. It is very important that only a very limited number of employees have access to these areas, and if video cameras can be installed in these areas, that is always a benefit.

Another way that theft can occur is by "short ringing" or "shorting" the house as it applies to sales of product. This is most easily seen in the bar area of a restaurant because there is a one-to-one relationship between the guest and the server (or in this case, bartender) and receiving your drink, whereas there is a multi-step process as it applies to ordering food. For food orders, the guest orders what they would like, and the server will enter that order into the POS system. That order is then printed up in the kitchen so it can be made, so there is not really a chance to be able to misrepresent what is being made.

For the bartender to make this work, some studying needs to be done in order to make sure the opportunity exists to be able to "short" the house. It works this way: a guest orders a drink that is a top-shelf or premium spirit cocktail. The bartender will make the drink, give that to the guest, and tell them the price. The goal is for the guest to pay, with cash, for the drink at the time their drink is presented to them. The bartender then accepts the payment and goes to the POS system to process the payment.

What the bartender has not done, however, is enter the ordered drink before making it. After the guest has tendered payment and the bartender has the cash in hand, the bartender rings in the drink that was ordered at that time. The key to this theft is that the drink rung into the POS system is not the drink that was ordered. The drink entered into the system would be one that used the house/well brand spirit as opposed to the premium spirit, and the change given to the guest is in line with the price of what the guest ordered with the premium spirit. The bartender can pocket the difference, and the guest would never know.

If done properly, on a day-to-day basis, this is tough to catch if the bartender does it smoothly, as the cash due to the restaurant at the end of the night is correct and there is not a trace of the theft on the daily financial paperwork. This would be seen, however, if a certain high-end beverage is moving off the shelves too quickly and the sales and the inventory does not support that should be the case.

In order to utilize this method, the person committing the theft needs to know that the person paying will be paying in cash and also does not need to see the check for the drinks they had. If the guest did need to see a copy of the check, the bartender would have to create a new check that showed the proper drinks ordered and then go back and void those drinks out, as that check would not be able to be closed since the other, the fraudulent ticket, is the one that would have been closed.

If this were to happen, then the manager should see these on the void report and be able to ask why the drinks were voided off. Again, if this is a one-time occurrence, it is hard to pick up, but if the same type of activity is showing up repeatedly with a specific employee, that should raise a red flag.

Where shorting the house benefits the person who is providing service to the guest, there are many cases where someone working in a restaurant takes liberties with the rules of the establishment, provides food and drink to their friends, and charges the guest less than what should be charged. This is still more difficult to do as it applies to food, but this can still be done.

If the server/bartender were able to move the food items

that were ordered to a comp line, such as "guest did not like" or "cooked wrong," the guest would not be charged for those items. For beverages, this is incredibly easy to do as it is just a matter of getting the guest another drink without ringing anything in through the POS system. This is, again, most easily done for guests who are dealing with a server/bartender in a one-on-one situation and there is nothing that has to get entered through a POS system (like any food order) so the kitchen is notified to create the order.

The payoff for the guest is obvious as they are paying for a fraction of what they ordered. In return, the gratuity amount left for the employee is usually greater than it should be. So in this scenario, the house loses product, and the employee makes money on the product being given away. This is noticeable if there are odd comps that are done to take care of the ordered food items, but it is tougher to notice this as it applies to beverage. Again, if there seems to be product that is being run through too quickly and the sales reports do not support the amount of beverage being used, that would be a red flag.

The hardest free item to pick up on would be the giving out of "free" draft beer. A standard 15.5-gallon size keg has 124 sixteen-ounce pours before a keg is empty, so if a server were to give away a few beers, it would be hard to detect, especially if your draft beer system can be temperamental and pour foamy beer on occasion. This would probably just get written off as spillage/waste as opposed to anyone suspecting that an employee was giving away free product.

Yet another way to try to beat the system and steal from the house is by manipulating the POS system as it applies to presenting the guest with their check and the close-out process of the guest's check. The key to this is knowing if the guest is planning to pay with cash. If that is the case, the way this works is that the server presents the check for the guest to pay at the end of their dining experience. Once the check is presented and paid, the guest is given back whatever change is due back to them.

Before the check is closed out in the POS system, the server will go into that check and void or comp off items in order to lower what is due to be paid to the house. The difference is the amount that the server can pocket. This type of fraud cannot be done without some level of participation by the manager, however. When items are moved off a check for the case of a void or comp, the POS system should ask for a manager's approval to ultimately clear that transaction out of the system. If the server has access to the manager's access code or swipe card, that is negligence on behalf of the manager, as this is something that should not be available to anyone except the manager.

If the server does not have access to a manager's code or card, then that check cannot be closed until the manager moves and clears those items off the POS system. At that time, the manager needs to ask the server about any items that were voided or comped off a guest's check and why that occurred. This happening on an isolated basis is not unusual, so this is not always an indication of theft. If this seems to always be happening with a specific server, that is when this needs to be looked at for theft.

Another form of theft that can be found in the hospitality industry does not involve actual cash from the guest, but it is an expense to the restaurant. This has to do employees and their use of their time on the clock, as well as their clocking in and out patterns. If you have a BOH employee who makes $20 per hour that consistently clocks in about fifteen minutes early and then also takes an extra ten minutes to clock out at the end of their shift, this would add up to over $2,000 per year in wages being paid out. If this type of behavior is consistent with an entire staff, it very quickly can balloon out of control where the house is paying out tens of thousands of dollars annually for time where no work is actually being done. This also makes it very difficult for managers to be able to keep their labor costs in line with set percentages that have been set into the annual budget. In addition to what would be just over two hours of time per week that the employee was getting paid for and not really doing any work, this could be the difference in an employee being pushed into overtime hours if they have to cover some extra time due to others being on a day off or vacation.

This type of behavior is common in the workplace, especially if it is never mentioned that the clock in/clock out policy would dictate that employees are not to milk the clock either coming in or leaving their shift. The majority of time clock programs are now built so they have a window of time that is allowed as a grace period at the beginning or end of a shift that if the employee does not clock in or out during their scheduled times, they have to get a manager's approval to override the clocking in/out process. This will allow the manager to stay knowledgeable of who is doing a good job with their clock in/out times and who is consistently working on the fringes of what is allowed. The manager should also be allowed to go back and edit times if there are employees who forget to clock out at the end of their shift.

The majority of POS systems will automatically clock out any employee who is still clocked in when the system does its daily backup, but it is still up to the manager to then go back and reset an employee's actual time. This is seen as a victimless crime as there is no actual money or product being taken from the restaurant, but this is the most common form of theft in the restaurant industry.

One of the final pieces to making sure that no overt theft is done when a cash drawer is turned in at the end of a shift. There are a few different methods that people use when counting out a drawer, but one that makes the most sense is taking out what the drawer's starting amount would be and counting down the rest of the money that is in the drawer. What is left in the drawer should match the register tape that is run, which would show all of the sales that occurred on that POS system for that shift. The payment transactions are broken down into the credit card payments and cash payments.

Each drawer that goes on the floor each shift should have a set amount that it goes out with. A normal amount is somewhere in the $300 range for most restaurants. At the end of the shift, the person(s) who have been on that particular POS system would print up the register tape that will have all of the day's data. This also will ensure that all of the checks that were opened on that POS have been closed. Once that is done, take out the initial $300 that the drawer had when it started. If the remaining money in the drawer does not match what the POS register tape says it should be the cash due for the shift/day, then the drawer is off. Each restaurant should have their own policy about how much a drawer is allowed to be over or under each shift. If a drawer is over by any amount, that amount gets pulled to the side, separate from the deposit for that drawer. You want the deposit for that drawer to match exactly what the register tape says it should be. If the drawer is short and within the allowable amount, the difference will be pulled from the house's petty cash in order to make the deposit match exactly to what the POS register tape says it should be.

If you have a drawer that is short by more than the allowable amount, the person(s) who handled that drawer are responsible for making the drawer whole. It could be a simple mistake where a guest was given incorrect change, so this is not always a sign of theft occurring. If certain employees seem to continually have drawers that are short of money, however, this could be a sign that there is some theft happening. One of the excuses commonly heard is that the employee just keeps their tips in the cash drawer. Whatever the difference is between the cash due at the end of their shift and the amount that the drawer is supposed to have to start the shift is the tip amount that is for the server. This is comingling of funds. This is not illegal, but it is irresponsible. Tips always need to be kept separately so there is no confusion between the money that is for the house and what the tips are for the employee.

When a cash drawer is counted down and all of the amounts are correct, then the amount that is the cash due for the day's sales needs to get pulled aside and combined with any other cash drawer amounts from other POS stations during the workday. These amounts are combined and made into the day's deposit. Depending on how your restaurant operates will dictate how that money gets to the bank for deposit. A copy of the deposit slip needs to be sent either manually or electronically to the person who handles the accounting for the restaurant to show that was the amount that was sent to the bank for a given day.

Part of the responsibility of the accounting department is to make sure that what is presumed to go to the bank matches what that bank claims to receive. This can be checked by doing the bank reconciliation (chapter 3). In order to make sure that what is being reported is correct, the reconciliation should be done on a daily basis. This way, if there is any discrepancy, it can be taken care of as quickly as possible.

It is not easy to put a stop to all theft in a restaurant, but if you know where to look, it is easier to see where there are existing areas that would allow an employee the opportunity to steal from the house and/or guest. This does take controls at the employee level as well as the management and accounting level, and there should be a check and balance process that helps point out where any theft could be occurring.

The points that we are looking at in this chapter are very simple:

- There is always going to be theft of some sort that exists. It is up to you to know where to look to see it. Some theft is not looked at as such—giving away a "free" drink or "topping off" someone's drink—but until there is another term for it, this is theft. This can quickly make a profitable location lose money, and we are wanting to stop that.
- Rules exist for a reason, especially as it applies to handling cash. It is important that everyone knows these rules and follows them. There are no exceptions.
- Always develop good check and balance systems. Everyone benefits when these are in place and followed.

CHAPTER 10

The Importance of Proper Budgeting and Forecasting

Now that you know how to look at your revenue, your COGS, and your expenses in relation to your P&L, you need to know how all of that stacks up against what you were hoping and expecting to do each reporting period. You might have a profitable month, but is it as profitable as it needed to be? In addition, sometimes you will have a reporting period where you will take a loss. This is not the worst thing ever if you have planned for it. Just hopefully it is the exception and not the rule for your restaurant. That is where having a working budget comes in to play.

A big part of trying to achieve financial success in your restaurant is making sure that you have set a good course for your managers to follow as they try to maximize the profits of the business. This can easily be tracked through the comparison of the actual data that is generated and compiled daily against the budget that is in place. If there is a budget in place that is a sound budget, then it will be easy to know how your restaurant is doing versus expectations, whether that is set on a weekly or monthly budget.

Most companies look at a budget as an annual plan that details how they believe they will spend money over the course of the year. Whereas this is true for restaurants as well, the budget is equally as important to detail how and when the revenue is going to be generated for the year. The easiest way to think of this, if you are not familiar with the budgeting process, is that your budget is your theoretical P&L for the year. Because this is the path you are setting for your managers to follow, it needs to be possible to achieve the numbers that you are building in for the year.

Several factors are in play when it comes to budgeting, and the better you know your market, the more accurately you will be able to build out a working budget. One of the main factors that needs to be looked at is the geographical area you are in. For this exercise, we are going to use the Atlanta area as our point of reference (mostly because I live there and it covers a large number of demographics).

Atlanta, like most large metropolitan areas, is widely diverse, and some of the factors that will need to be looked at when knowing your target market are the area's growth rate, the median age, median income, overall employment status, and gender percentage. All of this type of information is easily accessible through public city records that can be found online.

Unless your restaurant is just getting started, there should be one or more years of sales information that will be available for use as historical data to be able to see trends on a year-over-year comparison. The more years there are to work with, the more accurate the trend analysis will be. Obviously you would like to see an increase in the sales/revenue on a year-over-year comparison, but even if there is a decline, that needs to be taken into account when building out your budgets. When looking at the year-over-year data, one needs to keep in mind that they are looking for patterns. If there is a steady increase or decrease in sales that stays relatively at the same growth percentage for several years, it is safe to assume that trend will continue. If there are large swings from year to year, there is still a reason as to why that would be happening. It could be that there are big events that are occurring in the area that drive sales one year but not the next. This is very common for cities that host large sporting events and conventions. That is also why it is important to keep records on the events that come to the area so you have a good working idea of what constitutes a good revenue year that has major events and what is a good year when there are less, or no, events, as you will need to plan for these. This type of information is available and easily found online through a city's calendar of events.

So from this point, you have established what the target market for your restaurant is, and you have historical data that shows how the restaurant has performed for (hopefully) several years. With that being the case, the best way to build out a budget is to build forward by working off the past. If the prior year were a normal year in so much as the establishment was not closed for any length of time, then the best way to approach the budgeting process is to just scale up (or down) from the prior year. It is not unreasonable to want to have all of your budget data entered into your accounting system by the start of December for the following year.

With that as benchmark, to properly pull together and review all of the budget information, you will want to give yourself a good six to eight weeks of time to build out what you are going to be entering as your budget. This will allow you to have a solid nine months of actual data from your current year to use to help build out your budget. This is ideal because you will know if there are any major events that will be in the upcoming year that did not occur in your current year or vice versa so you can scale up or down as needed.

The best place to start then is by setting the budgeted revenue for the upcoming year. You would want to start with the revenue because once that is set, you will be able to arrive at what your total sales will be for each month. Once you have that total sales number to work with, you will be easily able to set your expense budget for your cost of goods and your other expenses. In setting up the revenue portion of your budget, you can use a couple of different methods for how you would like to have your sales reported.

You will want to separate your food sales from your beverage sales, but from there, you have a few options on how much further you want to separate these categories. You can separate the lunch sales and the dinner sales for both food and beverage revenues. Within the beverage section, you can also separate out the liquor, beer, and wine sales. This is recommended because this will allow you to accurately show what the cost of goods is for each of the liquor, beer, and wine categories.

Since you are working with actual reported numbers from the prior year to help figure out what your revenues are going to be, you will need to figure out the percentage that you will want to scale up (or down) for calculating what your budgeted revenues will be. For this exercise, we will say that the scale up will be 2.5 percent from the previous year. That would mean that if your food sales for a prior year's month was $68,000, the budget amount would be $69,700 when scaled up by the 2.5 percent. This will need to be done for your food sales as well as your liquor, beer, and wine sales.

Once you have established what you believe your sales to be, it is very easy to set your COGS amounts (food and beverage costs) as you are just taking the sales numbers for those categories and multiplying the sales amounts by the cost of goods percentage that you are wanting to achieve.

For example, if your food revenue is $75,000 and you want to run a 31 percent food cost, your budget for your COGS for food would be $23,250. For the beverage part of figuring out your COGS, you can either have that as a combined (blended) number or separated out by the liquor, beer, and wine categories. The method for coming up with the budget numbers is the same process as for calculating the food numbers: you will take the revenue numbers for all of the beverage sales and multiply that by the overall percentage that you would like your blended beverage cost percentage to be.

If you want to split out liquor, beer, and wine, the process is the same as you would take the liquor sales and multiply that by the desired liquor cost percentage to get your COGS. The same will apply for beer and wine costs. Once the COGS are arrived at, you will have your gross profit numbers, as you just subtract the cost of goods sold from the total sales to arrive at the gross profit number.

Now that the revenue and cost of goods portions of the budget have been created, the next part is to fill in the other expenses in order to complete the budget. There will be some expenses that are set expenses that are the same amount every month. Examples of these types of expenses would be items like rent, cleaning service, and pest control. Since these expenses will be the same each month regardless of sales, the best thing to do is to fill in those amounts for each month of the year.

After that, the majority of the remaining expenses are all going to be based off a percentage of the total sales. Most accounting programs will have that percentage information on a standard P&L from the prior year. If it does not, then simply export a P&L statement into Excel and run a formula that will calculate the expense percentage against the total sales amount.

Once you have the percentage of what each of the expense lines was versus the total sales, evaluate those numbers to make sure they are a sound percentage. If you see that the expense from the prior year was either too low or too high, make the adjustment to the percentage for the current budget. In addition, take a look at the expense lines that may have had either a budgeted amount and no (or very little) expense reported for the year or, conversely, had activity throughout the year but no budget entered.

If that is the case, identify if it is a matter of a new expense line being introduced in the previous year or if there were a change in the expense coding that occurred. An example of something like this would be if you had budgeted for PR/marketing but see that there is expense showing up for advertising. Perhaps the advertising amount had been originally entered as part of the PR/marketing expense and it was decided to show advertising separately so that expense line was added at a later time. Either way, the budget should be set so that every expense line that had substantial activity should have a budget amount set.

So now that you have built out the basic structure of your budget, you will want to go back through and review what you have to make sure that it both makes sense and accurately reflects what you believe the upcoming year to be like financially. One of the main points to remember is that your budget is a reflection of what you believe the whole year is going to look like, not just one particular month. It is entirely possible that you will have a month or more that will actually be months where the restaurant loses money. This does not mean that the month was a failure. There are plenty of times where it can be expected that there will be a month where the outcome will be a negative month.

Referencing Atlanta again, during the summertime it gets incredibly hot and is not seen as a destination for conventioneers. There are usually not a lot of other events that would draw people to the downtown area. There are still going to be all of the expenses that normally occur, and in some cases, like utilities, there might be a spike in the expense due to having to run the air-conditioning at a higher usage rate. The labor costs will still exist, as will the rent, taxes, and food and beverage purchases.

This is where having an accurate budget is important. By comparing to at least one prior year and more, if available, you will be able to see what the trends are through the slow months. You will know to order less food and beverage because the expected revenues are going to be down, as there is no need to have items sit as inventory when they are not needed. It is also important to look at other factors that will impact the way that a month is going to go as it relates to the calendar. The manner that the holidays fall on the calendar can make a big difference on a year-over-year basis.

For example, if the Fourth of July falls on a Saturday, outside of maybe the Friday beforehand, there usually is not a great deal of office closures and people taking a few days off. If the holiday were to fall on a Wednesday, however, that can make a big difference in people taking some vacation time and going out of town. This would be an event that could directly affect the number of guests who are available to be visiting your restaurant that week.

Another area to look at when putting together a budget would be large events that happen annually or on a rotating basis that have a major impact on a whole area. Again, taking the Atlanta area as the example, when the NFL schedule is announced each year, the weeks that there are home games will vary from year to year and will have a profound influence on what a month's revenue could look like from one year to the next. The best way to work around this is to be able to figure out about how much of a difference a home game event makes in revenue versus a week where there is not a home event.

Using that as a scale, when the schedule is announced, knowing how much a home event is worth, that will need to be factored into your budget. The issue that can arise around a situation such as this is that the schedule release date is done in the summer and your budget for the year would already be completed and loaded into your accounting system.

This is where the reforecasting comes in to play. You already have a working idea of how much revenue will be generated by a full football season, but you won't know until midway through the year how the schedule affects the months of September, October,

November, and December. It is perfectly fine to do a reforecast
when there is information that comes to light that was not previously known. That is why the introduction of the dates of a football season's schedule is the perfect example of why reforecasting
occurs. You know that there will be eight home games so you
can figure out how much those are worth, but you just cannot be
certain which months are going to benefit as it applies to when
the revenue will show up.

There can also be reforecasting that needs to take place when
outside events occur that change the way your annual budget is
structured. It could be something like a large convention in the
area being canceled due to inclement weather. Through no one's
fault, large amounts of conventioneers and foot traffic or planned
events suddenly, on very short notice, do not exist. This type of
circumstance does come up, and they impact a budget that has
been set in place on both the revenue and expense side.

A final budgeting factor that comes into play is when there
are recurring events that happen in several-year intervals. Again,
using the Atlanta model, the downtown Atlanta area hosted a
Final Four in 2013 and will be hosting one again in 2020. For a
situation like this, if your restaurant was around at the time of
that previous event, you would want to take that very specific,
actual data and work that into a current budget. What you are
trying to accomplish by referencing this historic data is that you
know what you ran for your food, beverage, and labor costs when
that event occurred previously.

If you ran good percentages for that previous event, you will
have an idea of what can be achieved and what it will take to reach
those numbers again. In order to properly reflect the increase in
both the revenues and expenses, however, you will need to figure
out what the inflation rate is for the time period in between the
two dates of the recurring event. Events that are on a national
level, however, can exceed the concept of seeing just an increase

in business as large corporate sponsors regularly finance events all across a metropolitan area, and most of the restaurants in that given area will be at full capacity for the duration of the event.

Creating a proper budget and reforecasting when needed will give your operators the information that they need to be able to plot a course that should lead to a successful fiscal year for your restaurant. The more knowledge that is available to the managers, the better. This way they can make a budget that will reflect what the actual year brings. When that level of budgeting is achieved, the results can be tracked, which should lead to sound financial planning on a year in-year out basis.

There were more specific examples brought forth in this chapter than the others in an attempt to show how the budgeting process needs to be done. Every restaurant has their own set of specifics that they will need to keep in mind when building a budget, but some concepts are universal to building a budget that we looked at. Those are as follows:

- Know the importance of year-over-year trends and in-corporate those trends into your budget. The more data you have to reference, the more accurately you can build a budget that will reflect what you believe the upcoming year to be.
- If you start with the revenue, it is easy to build out the cost of goods sold and the other expenses for the remaining part of your budget. Since you have percentages that you want to target for your food, beverage, and labor costs, by applying those percentages, you will be able to set what the acceptable expenses would be for a reporting period because it would be in direct relation to your revenues. For the remaining expenses, you can reference past years to see what percentage of the total sales each expense category is and then set your budget to reflect

what you think will be the proper percentage of the total sales for future reporting periods.

- Your budget should act as what you believe your P&L for the year should look like at the end of the year. It is ok to have some reporting periods show a loss if that has been the trend in past years. If there are incidents that occur throughout the course of the year, either positive or negative, those can be reflected by doing a reforecast.

Conclusion

Well, we certainly covered quite a bit of material over the previous chapters, and hopefully you can apply some of these topics to your restaurant. Remember, your goal in all of this is to run a profitable enterprise. It is, however, much easier to find ways to lose and waste money than it is to make money in the hospitality industry. Being able to be profitable starts with one simple concept: you need to get customers to come and spend their money on your product. Once the customer has visited your establishment for the first time, if they return is now completely up to you, so make sure you give them a reason to want to come back.

Some return guests do so as a matter of convenience. As they say in real estate, "location, location, location." If you are fortunate to have the best location in your given area, take advantage of that. Do not take for granted the fact that it is easy for people to get to you. It is now easier than ever to get from point A to point B, so if you already have a captive audience, give them a reason to come see you as opposed to wanting to go somewhere else. Chances are, you are not the only option in your town when it comes to their dining and drinking choices.

Now that you have people coming to see you, give them the best experience that you can. This has to do with both what they want to eat and/or drink as well as the service provided to them. If they are happy with the dinner they had and feel like they got what they paid for, then that is always a good thing. If they feel like their server really took great care of them, anticipated their needs, and gave them an enjoyable experience, that is also a good thing. When you put those two concepts together, now you have laid the groundwork for a loyal customer. By gaining a loyal following of customers, you have accomplished a few goals. You have set yourself up to have a repeating revenue source, and you have helped your marketing and advertising without having to spend any money to do so.

As we have covered earlier, if you have a happy guest, they have the potential to tell others and help increase the number of people who want to come to your establishment. With the access available on social media, it is easy to let others know what you think of anything, let alone a restaurant.

Conversely, it is just as easy for someone to say what they did not like about your establishment and say every reason why they do not think that anyone should go there. Keeping that in mind, it is always important that every guest is treated with the highest level of care. Understandably, sometimes things just go wrong. That is to be expected in the industry. How you handle these challenges can be the difference between earning a guest's loyalty and return service or losing their business forever. Hopefully you won't experience too many of these challenges along the way, but they can and will happen. I promise you that.

So hopefully you have found the best location, have the right concept, and produce great food and drink served by an intelligent, pleasant staff and the revenue is rolling in. You are on your way. Just remember that having a good revenue stream does not guarantee profitability. We have gone through a number of different areas where your business can be losing money, and we have detailed some of the methods that can be put in place to keep that from happening. It is only natural to not know everything about the restaurant business right away. Through proper training and experience, you will be able to learn what does and doesn't work as it applies to profitability. One of the keys to gaining more proficiency in how to run a profitable operation is to seek out what you don't know and familiarize yourself with that information. Don't stop asking questions. As I have stated earlier, one of the big issues that restauranteurs encounter is that they don't know what they don't know. It is very difficult to put a plan into action when you are not sure what action to take.

The goal of this book was to help show you some of the areas that can ruin the profitability potential of a restaurant. Some of these topics were items that are fairly obvious while others were a bit more obscure and learned through years of experience in the hospitality field. Not all of these examples will pertain to everyone, but some general underlying concepts are common throughout the restaurant industry, regardless of where you are located and what your concept is. It is perfectly natural to avoid areas of the business that you do not understand or don't make sense to you and focus on the areas of the business that you are comfortable with. I am going to ask you to try to change that mind-set. If there is an area of the business that you know very well and are comfortable doing, I am going to urge you to save those tasks until later and do those when everything else is done (if possible).

Find the areas that you are not strong at and work on getting better at those. Anyone can be a smart, witty, intelligent person, but by actually learning to do a task that you are not familiar with, you will gain experience. When you take that experience and couple that with all of your other strengths, you will gain proficiency and skill. Over the course of time, that proficiency and skill will become wisdom, and you will be able to pass that along to others so they can pick up where you leave off and continue to move forward. Embrace what you don't know, and use those areas as your goals to always strive to be the best you can at making your restaurant profitable.

I am going to end by saying the same thing I started with. Owning and/or running a restaurant or bar is hard work. Anyone who tells you otherwise is not being completely honest with you. This book is not going to make it so there is less work to be done or suddenly make everything easier, but hopefully it will help you make it more profitable. (And if things are easier for you, then that is good too.)

Thanks for reading, and best of luck.

Appendix

When dealing with a daily sales report, there should be a break-down of the sales by category; payment (by method); comps; admin fees, which would be a sales manager commission or other similar fees; any sort of deposits that may have either been taken in for a future event or a deposit amount that was taken in that is now being applied to the actual event; the purchase and redemption of any gift cards; and the taxes collected on the daily sales. The following is an example of what the information in a DSR could look like:

Visa	$2,035.48
Mastercard	$220.97
Amer. Express	$547.57
Discover	$21.49
Total credit card	$2,825.51
room charges	$0.00
deposits taken	$0.00
applied deposits	$0.00
taxes	$222.68
food revenue	$1,978.75
NA beverage	$48.75

Liquor revenue	$199.00
Beer Revenue	$719.65
Wine Revenue	$106.00
Total Sales	$3,052.15
Gift card purchase	
Gift card redeem	-$8.10
open discounts	
employee food	$148.63
manager meals	$416.70
did not like	$12.25
kitchen error	
server error	
owner comp	
marketing	$82.75
Total Comps	$660.33
Admin fees	$64.00
tip out	$12.15
cash due	-$142.96
debits	$3,342.88
credits	$3,342.88

One of the items that may stand out is the fact that the cash collected from this day was a negative amount. The way that a negative cash amount is arrived at is that the amount of tips on the credit cards is greater than the cash brought in for the shift. In order to pay out all of the tips to the servers, there will be money pulled from the petty cash holdings (which should be in the safe), and that will take care of the servers being paid out properly. If there are constantly days of negative cash, at some point there will have to be a reloading of the petty cash amount, and that will need to be coordinated with a withdrawal from the bank.

To further illustrate how the DSR works, it also is important to know what makes up the debits and credits. The following is a color illustration of what would make up the debits and credits in this particular example:

Visa	$3,535.48
Mastercard	$220.97
Amer. Express	$547.57
Discover	$21.49
Total credit card	$4,325.51
room charges	$0.00
deposits taken	$0.00
applied deposits	$0.00
taxes	$222.68
food revenue	$2,978.75
NA beverage	$48.75
Liquor revenue	$399.00
Beer Revenue	$719.65
Wine Revenue	$106.00
Total Sales	$4,252.15
Gift card purchase	
Gift card redeem	-$8.10
open discounts	
employee food	$148.63
manager meals	$416.70
did not like	$12.25

kitchen error	
server error	
owner comp	
marketing	$82.75
Total Comps	$660.33
Admin fees	$64.00
tip out	$12.15
cash due	-$142.96
debits	$3,342.88
credits	$3,342.88

In addition to knowing what makes up the debits and credits, it is also important to know that when there is a change to a line item that is a debit, there must be a change to a line item that is a credit. Here is an example that has some changes made from the original DSR that we have been looking at:

Visa	$3,535.48
Mastercard	$220.97
Amer. Express	$547.57
Discover	$21.49
Total credit card	$4,325.51
room charges	$200.00
deposits taken	$1,500.00
applied deposits	$1,000.00
taxes	$222.68

food revenue	$2,978.75
NA beverage	$48.75
Liquor revenue	$399.00
Beer Revenue	$719.65
Wine Revenue	$106.00
Total Sales	$4,252.15
Gift card purchase	
Gift card redeem	-$8.10
open discounts	
employee food	$148.63
manager meals	$416.70
did not like	$12.25
kitchen error	
server error	
owner comp	
marketing	$82.75
Total Comps	$660.33
Admin fees	$64.00
tip out	$12.15
cash due	-$142.96
debits	$6,042.88
credits	$6,042.88

You will note that I have added some figures to the area of room charges, deposits taken, and applied deposits. By making changes to each of these lines, an offset must occur in order to keep the transaction in balance. For the room charge, we now see that there is $200 that was charged to someone's room, which in this case was a private party, and they bought $200 worth of liquor drinks, which is why you will see an increase of $200 for liquor revenue. This keeps the debits and credits in balance since the liquor sales gets posted as a credit and the payment, in this case to the room, is a debit.

As we continue, we see there was a deposit taken for a future event. You will see a $1,500 increase on the Visa line as well as a $1,500 increase on the deposits taken line. This stays in balance because the payment on the Visa is a debit (for money coming in), and the offset of that has to be a credit, which the deposit taken line is. Finally we see that there was an increase of $1,000 on the applied deposit line. Because this was money taken in advance for an upcoming event, when it is applied as payment, that will always be a debit. In this case, we also see the corresponding credit for $1,000 in an increase in food revenue. Again, the debits and credits balance, and your daily sales activity is able to be posted.

Since you know that each day's activity needs to balance in the amount that is going to the debits and credits, respectively, if your accounting system automatically brings in the daily information from the POS system, then this data will just need to be posted each day. Then it is part of the reporting data. If your system does not do an auto-import, then a journal entry will need to be done to bring that data in. For the original DSR information listed above, the journal entry would look as such:

	debit	credit
cash		$142.96
Visa	$2,035.48	
Mastercard	$220.97	
Amer. Express	$547.57	
Discover	$21.49	
open discounts		
employee food	$148.63	

manager meals	$416.70
did not like	$12.25
kitchen error	
server error	
owner comp	
marketing	$82.75
applied deposits	
gift card redeem	$8.10

room charges	$0.00
deposits taken	$0.00
taxes	$222.68
food revenue	$1,978.75
NA beverage	$48.75
Liquor revenue	$199.00
Beer Revenue	$719.65
Wine Revenue	$106.00
Admin fees	$64.00
tip out	$12.15

$3,493.94 $3,493.94

If the debit and credit amounts do not match, then something is not reporting or is mapped incorrectly. You cannot post a DSR entry that is out of balance, as the system will not let you.

For reconciliation purposes, what you would see on you daily amounts to clear would be two credit card amounts, one for the American Express and the other amount the combination of the other credit cards that are accepted. For this date, you should see something like the following:

Debit			
$2,277.94	Visa/MC/Dis	7/3/2018	☐
$547.57	Amex	7/3/2018	☐

To the right of the date would be a check box that you would be able to click on as these amounts post to the bank. Since the cash amount was negative, you would not see any cash total as a reconciling item. Once there is a deposit that would go to the bank, you will be looking for that total to show as a reconciling item. Since it is a cash deposit, it will show up in the reconciliation module listed as cash. The amount being deposited should be able to be tied back to the DSR(s) that represent the activity for the number of days that make up the deposit.

The chart of accounts is broken into several sections. The first division of the chart of accounts is between items that fall on the balance sheet and those that go to the P&L. The balance sheet, which we have not spent too much time on in this book, is a statement of the assets, liabilities, and capital of your business at a particular point in time. This details the balance of income and expense over the preceding periods. Some of the categories that make up the balance sheet are cash, accounts receivable, inventory, other assets, fixed assets, accounts payable, and current liabilities. When looking at your chart of accounts, the balance sheet accounts are (almost) always listed numerically before the P&L account numbers. An example of what a balance sheet section of the chart of accounts is as follows:

Account Number	Description	Account Type	Statement Type	Statement Category	Standard Balance
1000	Cash	Financial	Balance Sheet	Cash	Debit
1010	Primary Bank Account	Financial	Balance Sheet	Cash	Debit
1020	Bank Account #2	Financial	Balance Sheet	Cash	Debit
1030	Bank Account #3	Financial	Balance Sheet	Cash	Debit
1040	Bank Account #4	Financial	Balance Sheet	Cash	Debit
1070	Merchant Deposit Account #2	Financial	Balance Sheet	Cash	Debit
1080	Checks Received	Financial	Balance Sheet	Cash	Debit
1100	Accounts Receivable	Financial	Balance Sheet	Accounts Receivable	Debit
1200	Food Inventory	Financial	Balance Sheet	Inventory	Debit
1210	Meat Inventory	Financial	Balance Sheet	Inventory	Debit
1220	Poultry Inventory	Financial	Balance Sheet	Inventory	Debit
1230	Seafood Inventory	Financial	Balance Sheet	Inventory	Debit
1240	Dairy Inventory	Financial	Balance Sheet	Inventory	Debit
1250	Produce Inventory	Financial	Balance Sheet	Inventory	Debit
1260	Bakery Inventory	Financial	Balance Sheet	Inventory	Debit
1270	Frozen Inventory	Financial	Balance Sheet	Inventory	Debit
1280	Grocery Dry & Canned Inventory	Financial	Balance Sheet	Inventory	Debit
1320	Beverage Inventory	Financial	Balance Sheet	Inventory	Debit
1330	Liquor Inventory	Financial	Balance Sheet	Inventory	Debit
1340	Beer Inventory	Financial	Balance Sheet	Inventory	Debit
1350	Wine Inventory	Financial	Balance Sheet	Inventory	Debit
1360	Merchandise Inventory	Financial	Balance Sheet	Inventory	Debit
1380	Bar & Consumable Inventory	Financial	Balance Sheet	Inventory	Debit

Account Number	Description	Account Type	Statement Type	Statement Category	Standard Balance
1400	Prepaid Expenses & Advances	Financial	Balance Sheet	Other Assets	Debit
1500	Fixed assets	Financial	Balance Sheet	Fixed Assets	Debit
1510	Land & Building	Financial	Balance Sheet	Fixed Assets	Debit
1520	Automobile	Financial	Balance Sheet	Fixed Assets	Debit
1530	Furniture Fixtures & Equipment	Financial	Balance Sheet	Fixed Assets	Debit
1540	Leasehold Improvements	Financial	Balance Sheet	Fixed Assets	Debit
1600	Accumulated Depreciation	Financial	Balance Sheet	Fixed Assets	Debit
1700	Capitalized Start Up Expenses	Financial	Balance Sheet	Fixed Assets	Debit
1800	Security Deposits	Financial	Balance Sheet	Fixed Assets	Debit
2000	Accounts Payable	Financial	Balance Sheet	Accounts Payable	Debit
2110	Credit Card	Financial	Balance Sheet	Current Liabilities	Debit
2120	Credit Card #2	Financial	Balance Sheet	Current Liabilities	Debit
2210	Sales Tax Payable	Financial	Balance Sheet	Current Liabilities	Debit
2220	Second Tax Payable	Financial	Balance Sheet	Current Liabilities	Debit
2250	Payroll Liabilities	Financial	Balance Sheet	Current Liabilities	Debit
2260	Second Payroll Liability	Financial	Balance Sheet	Current Liabilities	Debit
2280	Tips held	Financial	Balance Sheet	Current Liabilities	Debit
2300	Gift cards & certificates	Financial	Balance Sheet	Current Liabilities	Debit
2350	Customer Credits	Financial	Balance Sheet	Current Liabilities	Debit
2400	Notes Payable	Financial	Balance Sheet	Current Liabilities	Debit
2500	Other debt	Financial	Balance Sheet	Current Liabilities	Debit
3000	Owner Capital	Financial	Balance Sheet	Current Liabilities	Debit
3100	Common Stock	Financial	Balance Sheet	Current Liabilities	Debit
3300	Retained Earnings	Financial	Balance Sheet	Current Liabilities	Debit

The chart of accounts will show the account number, description of what the account is, what type of account it is (financial or other), statement type (balance sheet or P&L), statement category, and standard balance. The standard balance is which side (debit or credit) of a journal entry you would put the number if you want to increase the value of that category.

The other section of the chart of accounts is for the accounts that are part of the P&L. The P&L (also referred to as an income statement) shows the revenues and expenses for your business for a distinct period of time. The chart of accounts section that is for the P&L will include the revenue (sales), COGS, and all other expenses. How far you break down what all the expenses (like repairs and maintenance or comps) are completely at your discretion. The following is an example of a profit and loss section of a chart of accounts:

Account Number	Description	Account Type	Statement Type	Statement Category	Standard Balance
4000	Sales Revenue	Financial	Profit & Loss	Sales	Credit
4200	Food Sales	Financial	Profit & Loss	Sales	Credit
4320	Beverage Sales	Financial	Profit & Loss	Sales	Credit
4330	Liquor Sales	Financial	Profit & Loss	Sales	Credit
4340	Beer Sales	Financial	Profit & Loss	Sales	Credit
4350	Wine Sales	Financial	Profit & Loss	Sales	Credit
4360	Merchandise Sales	Financial	Profit & Loss	Sales	Credit
4500	Catering & contracts	Financial	Profit & Loss	Sales	Credit
4700	Other Operating Income	Financial	Profit & Loss	Sales	Credit
4900	Discounts	Financial	Profit & Loss	Sales	Credit
5000	Cost of Sales	Financial	Profit & Loss	Cost of Sales	Debit
5200	Food Cost	Financial	Profit & Loss	Cost of Sales	Debit
5210	Meat Cost	Financial	Profit & Loss	Cost of Sales	Debit
5220	Poultry Cost	Financial	Profit & Loss	Cost of Sales	Debit
5230	Seafood Cost	Financial	Profit & Loss	Cost of Sales	Debit
5240	Dairy Cost	Financial	Profit & Loss	Cost of Sales	Debit
5250	Produce Cost	Financial	Profit & Loss	Cost of Sales	Debit
5260	Bakery Cost	Financial	Profit & Loss	Cost of Sales	Debit
5270	Frozen Cost	Financial	Profit & Loss	Cost of Sales	Debit
5280	Grocery Dry & Canned Cost	Financial	Profit & Loss	Cost of Sales	Debit
5320	Beverage Cost	Financial	Profit & Loss	Cost of Sales	Debit
5330	Liquor Cost	Financial	Profit & Loss	Cost of Sales	Debit
5340	Beer Cost	Financial	Profit & Loss	Cost of Sales	Debit
5350	Wine Cost	Financial	Profit & Loss	Cost of Sales	Debit
5360	Merchandise Cost	Financial	Profit & Loss	Cost of Sales	Debit

5380	Bar & Consumable Cost	Financial	Profit & Loss	Cost of Sales	Debit
5600	Delivery & direct labor Cost	Financial	Profit & Loss	Cost of Sales	Debit
5700	Merchant Fees	Financial	Profit & Loss	Cost of Sales	Debit
6000	Labor related expenses	Financial	Profit & Loss	Salaries and Wages	Debit
6100	Management Wages	Financial	Profit & Loss	Salaries and Wages	Debit
6200	Staff Wages	Financial	Profit & Loss	Salaries and Wages	Debit
6300	Contract Labor	Financial	Profit & Loss	Salaries and Wages	Debit
6400	Commissions paid	Financial	Profit & Loss	Salaries and Wages	Debit
6500	Employee Benefits	Financial	Profit & Loss	Employee Benefits	Debit
6600	Workers Comp Insurance	Financial	Profit & Loss	Employee Benefits	Debit
6700	Employers Payroll Taxes	Financial	Profit & Loss	Employee Benefits	Debit
6800	Payroll processing expense	Financial	Profit & Loss	Employee Benefits	Debit
7100	Direct Operating Expenses	Financial	Profit & Loss	Operating Expenses	Debit
7110	China - Glassware - Flatware	Financial	Profit & Loss	Operating Expenses	Debit
7120	Restaurant & Kitchen Supply	Financial	Profit & Loss	Operating Expenses	Debit
7130	Cleaning Supply & Expense	Financial	Profit & Loss	Operating Expenses	Debit
7140	Decorations & Guest Supply	Financial	Profit & Loss	Operating Expenses	Debit
7150	Laundry - Linen - Uniforms	Financial	Profit & Loss	Operating Expenses	Debit
7160	Fees - Permits - Licenses	Financial	Profit & Loss	Operating Expenses	Debit
7200	Pest - Security - other contract	Financial	Profit & Loss	Operating Expenses	Debit
7250	POS - Tech support - Online serv	Financial	Profit & Loss	Operating Expenses	Debit
7300	Marketing	Financial	Profit & Loss	Operating Expenses	Debit
7310	Media & Print advertising	Financial	Profit & Loss	Operating Expenses	Debit
7320	Promotional events	Financial	Profit & Loss	Operating Expenses	Debit
7400	Automobile & travel	Financial	Profit & Loss	Operating Expenses	Debit
7500	Music and Entertainment	Financial	Profit & Loss	Operating Expenses	Debit

All of the same detail maintains for this section of the chart of accounts as it does for the balance sheet section of the chart of accounts in relation to the account number, description, account type, statement type, category, and standard balance.

Every restaurant should have an employee handbook that would detail the responsibilities for both the FOH and BOH procedures. This should include both opening and closing procedures for both the FOH and BOH. The following lists some of the more common duties for both the FOH and BOH for opening the restaurant and closing down at the end of the day. Each location will have tasks that are required that are unique unto them, but these items are fairly standard for all locations.

FOH Opening[18]

- Make sure that the dining room area is clean and the tables, chairs, and booths are set as needed.
- Stock up and clean any condiments.
- Using glass cleaning, make sure that all glass doors, windows, and display cases are clean.
- Check the host stand. Make sure it is clean and stocked as needed.
- Make sure all POS printers are working and have paper.
- Make sure that all credit card printers are working and have paper.
- Verify that all of the bathrooms were cleaned as part of the closing list of items that need to be done. If something were missed, take care of that before opening.
- Verify that the soda gun was soaked overnight, and reassemble the gun for the day's use.
- Check to make sure that the ice bins are fully stocked with fresh, clean ice.
- Make coffee as needed.
- Prepare any condiments that will be used on the floor, such as lemons for drinking water.
- Have sanitation buckets of water prepared and have towels ready for use as well.
- Make sure that there is plenty of silverware ready for use.
- Clean and prepare any food prepping that is related to the server area.
- Verify the seating chart has been done for the shift.
- Stock up on replacement linens for the tables so linen changes can be done quickly.

---

[18] "Server Opening Checklist", workplacewizards.com, accessed August 9, 2019, http://workplacewizards.com/picture/server-opening-checklist-large4-%2004-05-2016.jpg

- Check all glassware for chips or breaks.
- Check tables and chairs for any wobbles.
- Verify that all lights are working properly.
- If there is an 86 list, make sure it is up to date.
- Make sure that room temperature/thermostats are at correct levels.
- Check the POS system is operational. If it is not, make sure you have proper backup systems ready to go.

FOH Closing[19]

- Clean off all tables, booths, and chairs. Change linens as needed.
- Leave tables in proper location if there were any seating rearrangement during the day.
- Clean and sweep floor of entry dining area.
- Ensure all silverware is properly stocked up and prepared for the morning shift.
- Clean any glass areas to remove any fingerprints or smudges.
- Stock up all condiments so they are ready for the morning shift.
- Clean and organize all countertops and shelves.
- Take out trash, clean trash cans, and use new trash can liners.
- Make sure the coffee station is cleaned and turned off and the proper supplies are stocked.
- Clean and sanitize all food prep areas.
- Cover and date properly any food that is stored in the area.

---

[19] :Server Closing Checklist", workplacewizards.com, accessed August 9, 2019, https://www.workplacewizards.com/restaurant-server-closing-checklist/?cn-reloaded=1

- Turn off and clean any food warmers or steam tray areas.
- Take apart soda gun and soak in carbonated water overnight.
- Make sure all sinks are cleaned.
- Take anything that needs to go to the dishwashing area while dishes are still being cleaned.
- Properly close out and clean POS terminals.

BOH Opening[20]

- Turn on hood vents and all applicable lighting.
- Set up the dishwashing area and silverware trays.
- Set up all sanitation stations with proper sanitized water buckets and towels.
- Take out any trash that may have not been taken out from night shift. Get trash cans in place and put in liners as needed.
- Turn on all of the grills, fryers, and cooking areas at the applicable time before opening.
- Pull all needed items from the coolers for daily setup. Make sure to check all of the date information to verify that the product being used is fresh.
- Make sure that all of the cooking utensils are in place for the shift.
- Replace and restock all items that were pulled for use from the coolers for the day.
- Make sure that all required food prep is started, and once the prep has started, ensure the food is kept in a proper storage area for use.
- Stock up all paper supplies that are needed for the day.

---

[20] "Restaurant Opening Kitchen Checklist", workplacewizards.com, accessed August 9, 2019, https://www.workplacewizards.com/restaurant-opening -kitchen-checklist/

- Be sure that all cleaning that needs to be done as the day progresses is done in a timely manner.
- Be sure to clean, restock, and prep as needed as you turn over to the night shift.

BOH Closing[21]

- Properly wash all dishes, glassware, pans, containers, silverware, cooking utensils, and lids and put away in their proper storage space.
- Clean and sanitize the dish area, and turn off all of the equipment as needed.
- Clean and sanitize all sinks.
- Take out all trash.
- Clean and restock restrooms for the following day.
- Clean and sanitize all surfaces of the cooking area.
- Properly seal, date, and store all food that needs to be stored in the coolers.
- Clean all coolers inside and out.
- Make sure that all food that is in cooler storage is rotated so all of the food is used before it expires.
- Take apart and clean all cooking and prep equipment (slicers, mixers, etc.).
- Break down and take out all boxes.
- Power down and thoroughly clean all cooking surfaces.
- Properly sweep and mop the floor.
- Verify that all of the coolers are working at the proper storage temperatures.

Author Biography

Stephen A. Mase has more than twenty-five years of experience in the food and beverage business. As someone who has seen and dealt with all facets of the restaurant business, he knows how to operate a profitable operation.